T0359326

WHAT I WISH I HAD KNOWN

RESISTING THE URGE TO LIVE

DASIA BLACK

Dr Dasia Black was born in Poland at outbreak of war. She was three years old when the Nazis marched into her township in Galicia. Dasia's parents were murdered by the Nazis. Escaping from Communist Poland with her adoptive parents, she arrived in Australia at the age of twelve, where she completed her schooling and university studies at Sydney University.

She is the author of two published books, *Letter from my Father*, a memoir in which she examined the impact of her parents disappearing from her life at the age of four and *Zbaraz. A Community Extinguished* , which follows the child's quest for precious details about her parents life and death.

For most of her professional life, Dasia lectured and researched at the Australia Catholic University on various aspects of human development and the psychology of racism. She was involved in a program of Teacher Education of Aboriginal students in their communities. Dasia is a proud grandmother of 5 grandchildren.

ISBN 9781761282249 (print)

Book production by:

Booktopia Publishing, a division of Booktopia Group Ltd
Unit E1, 3-29 Birnie Avenue, Lidcombe, NSW 2141, Australia

Printed and bound in Australia by Pegasus Media & Logistics

The paper in this book is FSC® certified.
FSC® promotes environmentally responsible,
socially beneficial and economically viable
management of the world's forests.

booktopia.com.au

To the memory of my son who took his life
at the age of forty-three, and to the bereaved parents
who trusted me and opened their hearts to me.

What is certain is that they all suffered beyond description, to the point where suffering has become a mental sickness. And as we bow in homage to their gifts and to their bright memories, we should bow compassionately before their suffering.

Boris Pasternak, from *An Essay in Autobiography*, 1959

Suicide: a terrible but utterly natural reaction to the strained, narrow, unnatural necessities we sometimes create for ourselves.

Al Alvarez, from *The Savage God*, 1972

Acknowledgements

At the heart of this book are the many letters I received from bereaved parents who lost a child, in most cases a son but in some cases a daughter, to suicide. Some respondents also wrote about a spouse or a sibling who took their life. These letters were a response to a note that I was encouraged to publish in the January/February 2019 newsletter of the Support After Suicide Group, for which I am most grateful. Their monthly newsletter had supported me in my darkest moments over the fifteen years since my younger son took his life.

My deepest gratitude goes to each one of the bereaved who opened their hearts to me and trusted me with sometimes graphic descriptions of the act of suicide by their loved ones; the context in which it took place, their anguish and above all, the question of what could have been done to prevent it.

My friend and well-known author Diane Armstrong generously guided me towards publication, offering wise advice and steadfast encouragement on many an occasion. She rejoiced with me at every step towards bringing this book to fruition. My friend Yola Center found time to proofread the book in her usual meticulous manner, as she had done for everything I had ever written. She did it at a time when she was herself under tremendous stress. As ever, I appreciate her discriminating comments.

Kim Slender, a scholar in the area of epigenetic transmission of trauma, introduced me to the field and patiently monitored my steps in gaining an understanding of this relatively new and yet most relevant research.

This book would not have ever been published without Selwa Anthony, my literary agent. I cannot thank her enough for her commitment, understanding and above all, belief in the value of the book. My deepest appreciation to Jon MacDonald of Booktopia.

It was a pleasure to work with my editor Glenda Downing. I appreciate her skills and gentle suggestions.

My thanks and appreciation to my partner David, who had to put up with my preoccupation, my ups and downs relating to the numerous aspects of writing a book and bringing it towards publication. Particularly challenging were my at times deep anguish and pain related to my own loss and also to that of my respondents.

And then there is my family – my son and daughter-in-law and my five grandchildren. Their love, their very existence, nourish and sustain me.

Contents

Introduction

My son Jonathan died by suicide on Saturday 8 January 2005. He had injected himself with potassium chloride. His body was not found until Monday morning, by the cleaner who entered his room at 6am.

He was lying on the floor with the computer still displaying a slide show of his children. At 9am that morning, two burly, yet gentle police officers arrived at our home and told the news to me and my late husband, Sam. This is not the place to describe my reaction and it is all very hazy, but a few hours later I was ushered in by the counsellor at the morgue to view Jonathan's body. He was intact and looked peaceful.

Jonathan was the younger of my two sons. At 43 years he was still my older son Simon's kid brother. I have written chapters of the devastating impact on me of my son killing himself, which one day may be published elsewhere, but I found a note I had written to a friend in Israel that caught my immediate feelings:

My dearest Liora

My dear friend, something terrible has happened. My darling son Jonathan's body was found this morning in his rooms in the hospital where he apparently went on Saturday morning. He may have died two days ago, possibly of a heart attack. The tensions of the last couple of years, with financial issues, his divorce, and the difficulties in seeing his children for no more than a couple of days every fortnight caused him enormous stress. He did not have the will or interest to start a new life. Medicine and the children were his life. He had lost weight, perhaps too much. However, he was not a man to show his emotions and kept himself very locked up. The children are in Melbourne visiting their maternal grandmother and will be coming back soon. Simon and his family are in Israel but are flying back. I went to see Jonathan's body in the morgue today and he looked so beautiful. I could not stop kissing him. He was such a joyous child, with extraordinary gifts. He had just had a few days with the children in Queensland. He had dinner with us on Friday night and seemed OK, though rather tired. I am attaching a photo of him with the children. I am writing in the middle of the night after a couple of Normisons to let me sleep a few hours. Nothing else to say.

The first few months following my son's suicide were a period of such severe anguish and shock that I doubted my ability to bear it. But I did bear it. Preoccupation with the event of his death and immediate circumstances surrounding it overwhelmed me.

In my total devastation there were many things I did to keep on living, and one of them was to write down in the greatest detail the events leading up to Jonathan's death. Above all, I was consumed with finding an answer to the one and only question: How did he come to the decision to put an end to his precious life? Why did he do it? The literal meaning of suicide is to kill one's self. That is what he did.

At the time of his suicide he was in the middle of divorce proceedings. He had separated from his wife just over twelve months prior to taking his life and moved to a small apartment in an arty part of town. Outside his work as a cardiologist in both a public teaching hospital and private practice, his main preoccupation in the last year of his life was the struggle to maintain regular access to his two children. He felt there was a danger of losing close relationships with his children or, more importantly, losing contact with them altogether.

Of course, after his suicide and increasingly with time, I questioned myself, as many a parent does, on why and how I, a mother sensitive to her children's state of being, and a psychologist as well, did not pick up the many red flags signalling the danger that I can now clearly see were there.

The answer is simple. I saw my son in distress but did not in my wildest imagination consider him at risk. I was ignorant, as are so many bereaved parents. I knew very little about suicide and had never thought of it as a subject that might be relevant to my life.

Over the years my understanding widened, and I came to appreciate the other multiple pressures on Jonathan. He was burdened financially, as he and his wife appeared to have over-spent on rebuilding their house, and the legal costs of separation and divorce proceedings were significant. Plus there were rumours that his hospital may be amalgamated and moved to another location, which would have affected him professionally. But all these pressures did not, in my mind, justify the drastic step of killing oneself.

So, fifteen years after the event, I felt I had written, thought, talked and suffered anguish for long enough to let the past rest. And yet, only now have I come to consider that trying to identify and blame outside circumstances are just part of the answer to the why. After all, suicide was not the only option for Jonathan, and I see men in similar situations make different decisions to allow for change and hope.

I experienced a powerful urge to explore and learn what research has to tell us about the young men – and that is the biggest category – who carry out successful suicides. I wanted to learn about some of the elements that make up the 'perfect storm' of complexity and contradictions that contribute to suicide (detailed by Dr Jack Jordan, as quoted in Support after Suicide Group (SASG) Newsletter, July/August 2019). Above all, I wanted some answers to the question of what we, as parents, family members and community, can do to stop what seems an unnatural act of a young person carrying out lethal self-injury.

This is the aim of this book.

In my attempt to identify the danger signs of a suicide that we as parents and as a community must include in our common knowledge, and which I wish I had known, I turned to the Support after Suicide Group (SASG) in the Department of Forensic Medicine, Sydney, that published my request in their excellent newsletter. Hoping perhaps other bereaved parents would share their thoughts on these issues and on others that I have not considered.

My son Jonathan, aged 43, took his life on Saturday 8th January 2005 by injecting himself with potassium chloride in his rooms at a public hospital where he was a resident medical specialist. The cleaner found his body early Monday morning, with the slides of his children still moving on his computer.

Like most parents I went through profound grief, anguish and despair and wanted to understand. The Support after Suicide Group Newsletter was invaluable.

Being a psychologist by training, I thought I knew what to do to be able to go on living with a sense of purpose. We memorialized Jonathan in a variety of ways; I wrote a little book, Letter to my Son, attempting to capture his living presence. I recalled my memories of him as a joyful child, knowing that with aging some of them would wane. I even gave a paper at a Trauma conference a few months later on the impact of trauma on a child, recounting my own traumatic experiences, including a reference to my son's suicide.

I am at present in a peaceful period of my life and I thought that it is time to turn away from the pain. As friends and family say: Enough already. Yet, paradoxically, I have a strong urge that I have decided to follow; the urge to explore the 'Why' and 'How' of a healthy young man, coming from a family of Survivors, can take his life. I want to go beyond my own story to those of others who also know the anguish. I have read the poems, accounts, letters published in the SASG newsletters over the last 13 years and thought about the common themes that emerge: the child, often a son most loved; not giving any indications of his state of mind; his tendency to have a high privacy threshold. In the background there is frequently a difficult breakup of a relationship, as in my son's case, compounded by other factors.

Apart from conducting research, I wished to hear from parents who had lost a child by suicide. The questions they would like answered, what they can tell me to give a direction to my search for understanding of what led to these young lives unlived.

I indicated that I would appreciate any thoughts, suggestions, feedback they may want to contribute to the search. Of course, everyone's privacy was to be respected unless they gave me permission to give their name but I expected most would prefer to stay anonymous. I would keep them informed of progress of my project.

My request elicited some insightful and generous responses, many more than I had anticipated. They came mainly from parents but also from spouses. The writers told me of their beloved children (mainly sons); of the means they chose to take their lives; the immediate context and their ways of coping after the devastation.

The letters widened for me the spectrum of issues involved in a young person deciding on and following through with the act of suicide. They encouraged me in my quest to at least partially answer the question posed by Nora, one of my respondents: Is there anything, anything at all I could have said or done that would have made them stay?

I shall be referring to my respondents' letters in this book, using fictitious names with the exception of one respondent who gave me permission to use hers. Each respondent sought an answer to the why: Why did he do it? Why do our sons think that this is an option – to end their life?

Apart from my own experience of Jonathan's suicide, my respondents' accounts and personal interviews provided real-life examples of what I have found in my reading of relevant literature and philosophy.

I now have a greater understanding of some of Jonathan's motives and their underpinnings, and that understanding has given me a sense of satisfaction and perhaps some glimmer of what one can do to prevent our young ones from taking their lives. So, though much of the book is a case study of the complexity of factors that may have contributed to my son's suicide, I hope that what I have learned will help other bereaved parents and family members understand their loved ones' act. I also hope that it will make those whose sons and daughters and close family members are in distress more alert to signals that they are at risk. Indeed, it is that knowledge that should be part of every community's understanding.

1

Suicide is Thinkable

Until now I have thought of the suicide of a loved son or daughter or spouse as something that is unthinkable. In fact, in my autobiographical book Letter from My Father, I referred to Jonathan's taking his life as unthinkable. What an ignorant belief.

I did not know that suicide, rather than road accidents, is the leading single cause of death in Australian men aged between 15 and 44. Nine Australians die every day by suicide. That's more than double the road toll. Seventy-five per cent of those who take their own life are male. Each year approximately 3000 Australians kill themselves.

I did not know that doctors are over-represented among successful suicides. Jonathan was a young man in distress, and a doctor.

In recent times there has been a dramatic increase in research into, and community discussion of, the scourge of suicide among our young people. The government has announced a national goal of achieving zero suicides, reflecting community alarm at the number of lost years of healthy life. The Australian Institute of Health and Welfare and the National Mental Health Commission are bodies publishing research on preventing lethal self-injury to inform our understanding and actions. Our national government has significantly increased funds for prevention of suicide in recent times.

These are valuable steps but, as yet, knowledge of what one can actually do to prevent a young or older person taking their life is quite inadequate. Colin and his son Simon Tatz, in their comprehensive book The Sealed Box of Suicide (2019), stated that while suicide has been part of human experience in most cultures, the biomedical model has managed to imprison it in recent decades. Suicide is commonly portrayed as a mental health issue, an inevitable outcome of mental illness, especially depression. Tatz & Tatz challenged the orthodoxies that 90 per cent or more of suicides are due to mental illness and depression. In their view, suicide is a social fact. It isn't a disease, nor an inevitable outcome of a mental illness. Suicide arises from the social order, not the world of medical disorder. The most astute psychiatrist cannot predict that a patient, no matter how depressed, will lethally self-injure the very next day after a consultation. At this stage, suicide is not an area in which one can carry out systematic observation and experimentation.

As Tatz & Tatz pointed out, statistics have yet to show that their analysis produces a better understanding of suicide than examination of individual case studies. This book attempts such a study.

As the national rate of suicide has increased by 3.7 per cent over the last decade, Tatz & Tatz bemoaned the fact that suicide has become predominantly the province of mental health workers.

An article appeared in the Adelaide Independent News, on 14 December 2018, titled "It's Despair, Not Depression that's Responsible for Indigenous Suicide". The article pointed out that even outside Indigenous communities, a diagnosed mental illness is present in only about half of those who die by suicide. A study examining suicides in Victoria between 2009 and 2013 found that 48 per cent of the 2839 people who took their own life had no history of mental illness diagnosis.

Suicide arises from the complexity of the human condition.

Persons deciding to take their life make a conscious or unconscious choice of the best possible practical solution to a problem, crisis or desperation that is perceived as intolerable. It is intolerable because they experience some intensely felt psychological needs that are not being met. I discuss this in Chapters 14 and 15.

Suicide, like most significant actions, cannot be devoid of context. It occurs within a social setting, a physical place, a cultural and religious milieu; a welter of connections that give one a sense of belonging. And all these factors interact with the personality of a specific individual.

Young people who take their lives come from all walks of society – rich and poor, highly educated and with low levels of education, urban and rural – irrespective of ethnic or religious group. No part of society is immune. The best parents, the most supportive families, can be touched by this tragedy.

The means of suicide reflect the particular context in which the would-be-suicides find themselves. My son, a cardiologist, had the professional knowledge that an injection of potassium chloride would result in immediate death. Iris's fifteen-year-old son was found in a very secluded part of the garden on their semi-rural property. Another 20-year-old in a rural community, borrowed a gun and shot himself, having left work and gone to the local fairground. My friend's 43-year-old son, in a small town, jumped off a high bridge. A 23-year-old city man took his life by heroin overdose. Rosie described how her 30-year-old son went into his parents' bedroom, locked the door, stepped into their closet and shot himself in the head. Another died by asphyxiation in his car in a remote location. A 28-year-old girl living in a beachside suburb, went to her customary spot on the beach, took an overdose and lay herself on her favourite blanket, to be found later that morning by a surfer. An older man, a doctor, took an overdose very early in the morning and sat himself in his car, parked in the garage, to be found many hours later.

Reading that paragraph may be gruesome, but that is what suicide looks like. Once people decide that they no longer want to live and are prepared to act, they do not want to be stopped. Successful suicides take place in private, when no one is around. It may be when parents or partner are out of the house – early morning or late night.

The death of a young person, of a child, cuts deeply into the lives of their family. The cut is even deeper, even more devastating for parents, grandparents, siblings, children of the suicide, friends, indeed the immediate community, when it is not due to an incurable disease or horrific accident but to a voluntary act. Suicide is against nature, against the most powerful instinct of all living organisms, that of survival.

The impact of the suicide of a child goes beyond bereavement and loss associated with the death of a loved one. This death is different. It has all the features of a trauma – an event that goes beyond the natural losses one suffers over a lifetime, such as loss of a parent or spouse/partner. Trauma refers to an event that is outside one's normal expectations of the ups and downs of an ordinary life. It is a personal holocaust. Recovery from traumatic bereavement takes a long time and it can only be partial.

Terry wrote in his letter: "No one saw it coming. Suicide had never touched our family before. How could I have known he was going to kill himself?"

All the letters reported what is generally known but not understood until one experiences the loss of a child by suicide: total devastation, in some cases depression, and even suicidal thoughts by the bereaved. The anguish expressed by each and every one was painful beyond all measure. I am quoting a recent note received by a friend, just six weeks after her 29-year-old daughter ended her life by overdosing:

"Another hard day I can't get out of bed … crying … saddened … how to make sense of not being able to have one more conversation one more hug one more life giving memory … tossing and turning last night … very alone … the grief is thickened with layers of regret and hopes that will never come true … oh Dasia ... I have to believe that I will recover … the pain will never go. I can't ever imagine a day when I will not think of my beautiful daughter."

Belinda Woolley in her book *If Only…*, tells of Alison, whose son died by suicide at the age of eighteen. Alison wrote: "The depth of emotional pain I felt was overwhelming, and it seemed to permeate my very essence" (p.57).

Among my respondents there are a number of cases of multiple suicides within the family – one sister following two of her younger sisters, a teenager following his brother. The ripples of devastation spread over a lifespan and across generations. Ewin Hannan reported in an article in The Australian (22 June 2021) that for each life lost to suicide, the impacts are felt by up to 135 people, including family members, work colleagues, friends, first responders at the time of death.

A major impetus for Colin Tatz to write a book on self-death in the last year of his life, was the discovery that a great-uncle, a grain merchant, had misread his accounting ledgers and, wrongly believing he was bankrupt, adjourned to his barn and hanged himself with his trouser braces. As Tatz & Tatz tell it:

> *"Uncle 'D' wasn't mentally ill: he simply couldn't face the ignominy of insolvency, a monumental shame. The point of the story was it took the family almost 50 years to reveal his manner of death, the skeleton in our closet" (p.5).*

In terms of the aftermath of a young person taking their life, the anguish of mothers is particularly acute. After all, we mothers give birth to a child and all our instincts are focused on protecting, nourishing and nurturing this child. So it is natural that when that child chooses not to live, we see it as our failure. Denise wrote that she:

> *"… felt that there must be something wrong with me as a mother. I failed. Associated with the sense of failure is guilt of what we should have known and done. I feel like my heart is shattered and there is no way that it can be mended because a huge part of it is gone."*

Penelope agonised:

"…this is probably the most troubling and disturbing question I am left with – in my efforts to give my youngest child space to go his own way, solve his own problems and forge his own path, did I make a terrible mistake? Should I somehow have reached more deeply into his troubled mind and tried to help him find answers that would have kept him alive and well?"

Another respondent kept asking why she didn't know her son was in such a frame of mind. Liz wrote how she keeps going over the last two years of her son's life searching her mind: "what we could have done better in helping him. I felt and still do feel useless, I let my son down."

In writing about the anguish of mothers, it occurred to me that I knew little about what fathers felt, as most of the letters came from mothers. Fathers tended to keep silent. Then, in *Woolley*, I came across a letter to his son written by Roger, a father of a 23-year-old son who suicided by hanging himself. He titled his chapter "When We Meet Again You Can Tell Me Why" and asked, "Why didn't we pick up the vibes, Rich, so we had a chance to prevent this tragedy?" (p.39). His heartbreak and guilt were as intense as any of the mothers'.

After Jonathan's suicide and increasingly with time, I questioned myself on why and how I, a mother, sensitive to her children's state of being and a psychologist as well, did not pick up the many red flags signalling danger that I can now clearly see were there. I sometimes think that Jonathan would not have suicided had he thought of the impact on me, but of course I was not on his mind at the time he decided on and executed his life-taking action. In terms of Tatz & Tatz's reference to 'the skeleton' in the family closet, the notion of suicide that still has a stigma attached to it, it is still often a skeleton in the family closet, arising from its history as an illegal act, which I discuss in Chapter 19, 'A Historical Perspective'.

Iris wrote of her anguish that she could not reveal to her family in the Philippines how her beloved son had died, due to the stigma attached to it, such as condemnation, judgement and criticism.

Katrina expressed it clearly after her son's death:

"I was taken aback by the heartless comments and judgements made about him from friends and relatives. If we can remove the stigma from suicide and mental health, people will feel much safer and will seek help. It may help us save our children".

Attitudes are very hard to change. Though we may express new ways of seeing things, the deep underlying beliefs, rooted in the history of one's society, still prevail. Parents bereaved by their son's or daughter's suicide know well the reaction of well meaning people to the word suicide.

There is still the expression of 'committing suicide', as in 'committing a crime'. It may be wise to stop using this history-laden term of suicide and instead use 'lethal self-injury'. It is helpful to see the increasing use of the term 'self-harm'.

I know myself my hesitation when people ask about the topic of this book, as I anticipate their discomfort at the word 'suicide'. So much harder than to say: 'I am writing about cancer.' Change of attitudes happens when a society is fully committed to it and all its institutions take it on board.

2

Red Flags

In the period before people suicide, they exhibit a variety of behaviours that indicate they are not their usual self. In hindsight, my respondents, and certainly I, can identify red flags indicating that our children were experiencing distress. We may have seen the distress but did not in any way see it as pre-suicide behaviour.

Iris wrote that only after her son fatally injured himself, did she become aware of her teenage son's extreme mental pain, thinking that on that fateful night he did not feed his chickens and did not come home, which was certainly not his customary behaviour. Douglas told his mother, who was in phone contact with him, that he could not sleep at night. His wife reported that she was concerned the night before his deed, when he was very quiet at the party they attended and then drove home quite erratically, which was atypical of him. Nerida found out from her son's girlfriend that her son started "acting weird" on the evening he fatally self-injured; they got into a fight and he threatened to kill her and then himself before she left. Stella's daughter, who took her life at the age of twelve, started self-harming a few months earlier. The parents sought help, but it was ineffective.

Looking back at the last two or more years of Jonathan's life and particularly his last six months, there were clear red flags that my son was at risk but I did not understand or have knowledge of the extent or implication of these risks. Joy also expressed her regret that her son "had total support from us and I just did not realise his pain."

In the days preceding his suicide, I was aware that Jonathan was not as focused and energetic as usual. He knew the hearing of his divorce case was not far off and then there was his son's bar mitzvah in four months. He spoke in a disheartened way about the party for the occasion and how it could be managed.

One of my respondents also noted that her son was so withdrawn: but I did not pay much attention to it.

The day before Jonathan took his life was a Friday. He joined Sam and me for dinner. We had also expected Sam's daughter and her family, but they could not come. Jonathan remarked that it was just as well they couldn't come, since he was rather tired. We showed him our new plasma TV, of which he approved, and we ate the traditional Friday night dinner. He told us that the week away with the children he had taken had been 'great', though tiring, and that he was on call at the hospital for the weekend.

He sat straight and tall in one of our big blue velvet-upholstered chairs, looking handsome and tanned in a white shirt, though rather thin. He declared: 'I have laryngitis – though systemically, I'm all right.'

Our dinner was interrupted a number of times by calls on his pager from the hospital, which he answered rather impatiently. It struck me that this was unlike him, since he generally talked to his patients and colleagues with great courtesy.

Then Simon phoned from Israel, where he was holidaying with his family. The brothers had a short chat and Jonathan went home. Before leaving, he took a pink booking form for the ski resort of which I was a member and told me he was thinking of taking the children skiing in the July school holidays.

That my son was irritable and stressed that evening was obvious. But there were other signals of extreme stress over a longer period, and certainly in the last few months of his life. The obvious red flag was weight loss. He was a tall young man, well built, and he tended to be slightly overweight. When he separated from his wife and moved into his apartment more than a year prior to his suicide, I had offered to cook regular meals for him to put in the freezer. He could have them on nights when he had worked late hours or was too tired to worry about getting dinner himself. His favourite food was spaghetti bolognaise or meatballs in tomato sauce. So I cooked and packaged his choices in plastic containers, which he took home at regular intervals to put in the freezer.

The system worked very well and he appreciated my offer. But in the last three or four months, he declined the packages as he claimed he still had a plentiful supply at home. At the same time his weight loss became obvious, though it took a while for me to see it, as with his height, he could carry it off. I was mystified and started 'nagging', as he put it, about him getting too skinny, but he just brushed my comments aside. How was I to know that he was taking appetite-suppressing tablets, which act as stimulants, to counter his low energy? In fact, we found a whole stash of the tablets in his briefcase on his death and one of his colleagues explained their side effects.

Since his medical training, Jonathan also had firm views on strict hygiene. He insisted that the plates in the dishwasher be placed in alternative spaces, as having them close together would hinder proper cleaning. He would carefully examine the use-by date on packaging and tins, and would not use them even if the due date was only a few days old. He tended not to interfere with my more relaxed attitude to this. But I was aware that in the last two to three months he became quite obsessive about this. One evening after dining with us, he took everything out of my pantry, examined the due date and finished up with nearly half of the contents in a pile ready to be thrown out. I protested but seeing how insistent he was, I dutifully took them down to the garbage bin.

Jonathan, my superb and reliable computer consultant, also took it upon himself to clean all sorts of 'garbage' from my computer, warning me never to reply to an unknown sender as this was equivalent to having unsafe sex. I know every consultant would say the same, but Jonathan's new and intense interest in my computer, so different from responding to my occasional SOS, was unexpected. I now understand he was trying to establish order in the areas that were under his control.

Jonathan had some close friends, especially one who was also a doctor, with whom he had shared his private life ever since their first year as medical students. They seemed to discuss everything – what electives to take and where to go to dinner, what celebrations they would have, girlfriend issues, what holidays to take. Somehow, upon Jonathan's separation, his friend distanced himself from Jonathan and did not respond readily to his calls.

Jonathan's father had also distanced himself from his sons many years ago, after our divorce and his remarriage. He certainly was not there to support his son during his first and only year after separation from his wife and moving into his bachelor apartment.

Simon and his wife Ruth stayed close to Jonathan and their home was always open for him and his children. But in response to our questions about what could we do to help during these difficult days of marriage breakdown, he replied: 'This I have to solve on my own.'

Of course, I was there for him night and day but he refused to open up about his deepest fears and feelings. In retrospect, they were obvious. As I write this, I wonder about us parents thinking that it is natural for our adult and teenage children, especially sons, to confide in us. Perhaps this is a fallacy, and one needs to look to their peers or non-immediate family adults to find about our children.

Katrina also talked about her son hiding his pain and depression from everyone. Roger wrote about a strong façade hiding his son's soft core. The notion of the 'suicide hiding his pain' occurs frequently. I expand on it in Chapter 12, 'High Levels of Privacy'.

At some time during that year, putting on my psychologist hat, I suggested to Jonathan that he complete the Life Stress Inventory, a test measuring the extent of stress a person is experiencing at a specific point in time. Stresses may arise from happy events such as the marriage of one's child or moving to a new house, as well as unhappy ones. The inventory is quite exhaustive, looking at stresses emanating from a number of areas, including personal and social relationships, and employment worries. It is a test I had used frequently in my practice and it gave a fair indication of the extent to which a person was at risk. The risk may include a variety of health issues: lack of control that may affect one's behaviour towards those close to one as well as at work, and potentially suicide. Jonathan's score was at the very maximum level. When I told him his score was so high that it was off the chart, we just looked at each other and laughed. We laughed! Looking back, I cannot understand this quite inappropriate laughter. Did it indicate that in our minds he was a superman who could take it all in his stride? That we had extraordinary resilience? That we were the ones who would overcome severe stress? 'We', meaning he and I. I was a survivor and in my mind so was my son. Perhaps we were just innocents. Who knows?

Three or four months before Jonathan took his life, I was experiencing a strange sensation. I was aware of it most of my waking hours, but especially when about to go to sleep or on waking. It felt as if a fine tube attached to me was draining energy from me, ever so slowly but consistently. It was the opposite of having a liquid drip of nutrients or medicines attached to one in order to restore one's health. It was most uncomfortable and unsettling and tiring. In some way I felt that I was carrying someone by supplying their energy needs by this mysterious remote method. I suspected it was Jonathan, though I never voiced it. At times I resented it. My habit is to try to explain and understand things, but here I can only report.

A similar sort of premonition was reported by Alison, who was at a dinner with friends before she knew that her son had lethally self-injured. She started to hear a clear voice in her left ear saying her son's name. It gave her a strong feeling that she should phone him, but didn't get around to it until it was too late (Woolley, p.52).

Having been aware of Jonathan's irritability, weariness and deep fatigue in the last few weeks or perhaps months of his life, I have nevertheless protested, up to now, that Jonathan was not depressed. I am now rethinking the issue. In the analysis of my respondents whose children killed themselves, the word 'depression' and/or 'anxiety' appear in most cases. My psychiatrist colleague considered Jonathan to have been profoundly depressed and suggested that he thought he was able to cover it up, at least to his patients and family, by taking appetitive-suppressing tablets, which acted as stimulants. They allowed him to keep on functioning. It would have been a great personal effort for him.

I recall a conversation I had with a female medical friend of Jonathan's at the funeral. She and her husband were holidaying at the same island resort where Jonathan took his children two weeks before his death and which he described on his return as being 'wonderful, wonderful'. She observed that Jonathan and the children were having a good time but that he looked very weary.

So yes, if I look at Jonathan's death from within the medical/psychiatric domain, he did suffer depression – a risk factor linked to suicide. His depressed state could be understood as a reaction to the accumulation of stressors and traumatic events in the last two or more years of his life. Since he was a most energetic, enthusiastic child and young adult, delighting in so many aspects of life – love, nature, music, art and literature – depression had been, in my mind, the least likely characteristic that one could ascribe to Jonathan.

Observing the red flags in our sons and daughters and partners does not appear to alert us to the possibility that they have the intent to end their life, will attempt to do so and actually do it. But even when they do very clearly express their wish to die, the concept is so unthinkable that we do not listen. So when one mother's 24-year-old son replied "I want to die," to the question about what he really wanted, the mother answered: "No, you don't. If you did, you would have succeeded after trying three times" (Woolley, p.14). What a brave woman to write about it, and what guilt so evident in all of us.

3

Is My Life Worthy?

I find the view of suicide as necessarily an indication of mental illness quite inadequate. It does not help us understand the soul of the suicide. It does not predict suicide. People can recover from depression. There are other options.

The theory of evolution tells us about the variety and ingeniousness of adaptation exhibited by living organisms in order to live and reproduce. The many tales of survival under extreme conditions are evidence that the fight to survive is the norm.

The French philosopher Albert Camus, in his book The Myth of Sisyphus, expressed it well:

> *"In a man's attachment to life there is something*
> *stronger than all the ills in the world. The body's*
> *judgment is as good as that of the mind's, and the body*
> *shrinks from annihilation. We get into the habit of*

living before acquiring the habit of thinking. In that race which daily hastens us toward death, the body maintains its irreparable lead" (p.6).

Choosing life over death is natural. Life is worth the trouble of fighting death. Suicide requires resisting this built-in urge that defines us living organisms.

So what stopped my son and all the other young men and women from surviving? From choosing life?

One of my respondents from the SASG wrote: "And I know that there is no answer because of our human brains and complex thoughts. True, but it does not stop one searching for some understanding of those complex thoughts and motives, conscious and unconscious."

Unexpectedly, I came across some insights in the field of philosophy. They made more sense to me than the ubiquitous labelling of those who die by suicide as having mental health issues. That is a label with no depth of understanding of the mind of a person who commits suicide.

Rebecca Goldstein, in her book Betraying Spinoza, discussed the philosopher's notion of personal identity:

"A person is committed, immediately and unthinkingly, to the survival and flourishing of that single thing in the universe that he or she is ... That is, implicit in being one-self is the commitment to one-self" (p.161).

Spinoza wrote about the automatic concern about a person's own being and his or her intent to do what they think it takes to further their wellbeing. His concept of conatus (a natural tendency, impulse or striving, the inclination of a thing to persist in its own being) tries to capture the mysterious connection a person feels with that one thing in the world which happens to be itself (Goldstein, p.161). According to Spinoza, that commitment, in all its myriad ways of manifesting itself, is irrepressibly me (p.181).

Further, "the experience of being successful in one's endeavour, to feel oneself flourishing, expanding into the world, is pleasure; and to experience a decrease in one's power to persist, to feel one's self diminishing, contracting out of the world, is pain" (p.179). As I read these passages, I immediately connected the notion of commitment to one's self with Jonathan losing that commitment. More than losing the commitment. Suicide is the killing of that one thing in the world which happens to be itself.

Is that what is in the minds of the young men and women who choose not to go on living? Do they think that their self is no longer worthy of commitment, of surviving?

What I clearly witnessed, in hindsight, in his last few months and possibly last two years, was my son's self-diminishing. I witnessed it but did not see its implications, and also felt helpless to do anything.

The one conversation that haunts me is when he asked me at our lunch two years earlier to celebrate his birthday: 'Am I really so worthless?' I remember being stunned by the question and ruminating about it for days, but I did nothing. Yet, what a clear indication of the erosion of his valuing of and commitment to his self, worthy to all but him. Lorraine thought that her son had lost sight of his importance in the world (Woolley, p.24) – loss of his sense of worth.

As I contemplate Spinoza's concept of conatus, what comes to mind is that Jonathan's primary commitment was the welfare of others. Not only did he choose medicine as a profession, with his patients telling about his dedication, but in his everyday dealings he took a disproportionate interest in the wellbeing of those around him. His secretary, Anne, wrote in her report for the police that Jonathan was the best boss she had ever worked for. She told how she was participating in a national competition at the time, and Jonathan was cheering her on and responding to any success with all his enthusiasm. He never boasted of his own achievements, though clearly he was ambitious and achievement focused. I witnessed his daily commitment or even over-commitment to the welfare of others. Perhaps a greater balance between love of self and love of others may have been healthier, indeed life-preserving?

My respondents referred to their sons as being kind and sensitive and did not blame others for their problem (Nora). Megan described her son, who suicided at age 34, as gentle and intelligent; Iris saw hers as kind and sensitive, as polite and respectful. Again, in Lorraine's account of her son, 'Toby's Journey Towards Suicide', she tells how at her son's funeral, his friend referred to Toby's gentleness and individuality (Woolley, p.27).

Spinoza's philosophical concept of conatus makes more sense to me in understanding the mental state of a person contemplating suicide as an option to free themselves from the pain of despair. It is hard to fathom the feeling of hopelessness associated with thinking of one's life as worthless.

One needs to look at the vulnerability-building external factors in the would-be-suicide's environment, in their immediate and wider context, as well as vulnerabilities within the individual to gain some understanding of the pain of self-diminishing.

4

Relationship Breakdown

There is no single cause of suicide. In the background of the young people who take their lives is a complex web of interactions between unmet psychological needs, their personal characteristics, specific circumstances that provoke the associated intense psychological pain, and the interactions embedded within a wider cultural and social context.

Suicide, as understood by psychologist Edwin Shneidman (1995), is a response to intense psychache – hurt, anguish, and psychological pain in the mind of an individual. Suicide has a purpose; it is intentional death. It has a reason. Each lethal suicide act is a complicated, conscious or unconscious choice of the best possible practical solution to a problem, crisis or desperation that that person perceives as intolerable. It is intolerable because they experience some intensely felt psychological needs that are not being met.

The stoic Roman philosopher Seneca, writing in the first century, wrote about 'rational suicide'. In his view, a person who found themselves in bondage to circumstances that were beyond their control, who felt enslaved by incurable illness or personal relationships or societal oppression, may well rationally have seen suicide as a doorway to freedom.

Whereas in Roman times suicide was seen as understandable and even honoured, contemporary scholars like Shneidman also see suicide as a solution to an unbearable problem, but one to be prevented, one focused on opening other solutions. In Western societies life is precious.

In terms of what drives a person to suicide, what context contributes to their sense of worthlessness, the one factor that stands out among my respondents and literature is the breakdown of a significant relationship, a relationship that is central to one's life. And it seems that men are particularly vulnerable and at risk during the period of separation and divorce a red flag and a contributing cause.

Sarah wrote about an argument with his new wife the night her son took his life. Another told about her son's break up of a relationship with his girlfriend the night before, having gone through a divorce two years earlier. At the time of his suicide, Rosie's 45-year-old son was going through a breakup of his marriage and the children were not speaking to him. Another reported that her son was in anguish when his daughter and her mother moved interstate. The immediate context of fifteen-year-old John was that he had just come back from a holiday with his father, his parents having separated. An older man, a professional, overdosed and sat himself in his car in the garage the morning after the evening he had an argument with his wife and she told him she was leaving him.

Relationship breakdown is painful and requires adjustment on a number of fronts, but many people do separate and go on to form new relationships and new life frameworks. What is it about these young men that made relationship breakdown intolerable? What is it about their family dynamics and social context that contributes to their vulnerabilities?

What I understand is they were the type of men who took responsibility for the separation, who saw it as a failure on their part. They did not blame others. As Nora described her 39-year-old son, a high achiever in most aspects of his life, as honest, with a strong sense of fairness and justice and did not blame others for his problems.

Terry wrote about her 34-year-old son as extremely loyal and highly regarded in his workplace and in his personal life. Everything he did he achieved the highest acclaim for and yet …

Feeling that one has failed in a central aspect of one's life, that one is ineffective, certainly chips away at one's sense of worth. It leads to a shutting down, as conceived by Spinoza.

I can now see how this applied to Jonathan. Thinking of Jonathan as ineffective appears quite illogical. In fact, the opposite would be true. He had been successful in nearly all aspects of his life – an outstanding scholastic record at school and at university, followed by a brilliant medical career. He was loved by his family, friends and colleagues. He was good looking, talented in music and had a highly developed sense of aesthetics. The realisation dawns on me that the breakdown of his marriage would have been the one area in which he would have considered himself a failure. Failure was outside the horizon of how Jonathan functioned in life. I know that at the time of his marriage, he was totally committed to a good, lasting marriage that would form the basis of a family and satisfy his deepest needs for connection. He had suffered the consequences of his parents' marriage breakdown and this was not going to happen to him, nor his children. I witnessed the many ways he adapted to whatever he saw as necessary in order to make the marriage work. Divorce for him would not have been envisaged, even at the cost of unmet needs. When the marriage broke down, all his energy, passion, appetite and ambition were aborted.

Being the highly principled man he was, Jonathan would have taken a disproportionate responsibility for the marriage not working. What is more, the dynamics of his marital relationship were such that he would have felt that whatever was wrong was due to his own failings.

In the same vein, my respondent Liz wrote about her son being married to a woman who was profoundly possessive and jealous and who made life very difficult for him with her demands, but still he blamed himself for the relationship breakdown. In his eyes, he had failed.

I can now understand better why Jonathan could not see himself forming a new relationship with a loving woman. In fact, when we mentioned that a young woman he had dated prior to marriage was interested in meeting up with him, he said: 'Yes, possibly. She is familiar, but it's not likely to work.'

In reality there are many factors that are involved in the breakdown of a marriage. The obvious one is that the two partners are just wrong for each other from the very outset or, as the partners go through their life stages they realise that a divorce is essential for their mental and emotional wellbeing. That is why under

Australian law there is the fundamental view of no-fault divorce.

Perhaps a much greater sense of failure would have related to my son's perception of his relationship with his children. With every fibre of his being he worked for doing what was good for them during the times they were together and in his arrangements for the future. Unfortunately, he misunderstood or was ignorant of the fact that initial distancing, and intermittent at that, from the non-custodial parent, which is usually the father, in the period following separation is not an unusual response by children during times of intense confusion and upheaval. They are also allowed to be moody just as they often are in an intact marriage. One needs to be patient and appreciate that it takes time for children to adjust to a new family structure. And in most cases they do. In the early days it is a time when counselling, especially of the non-custodial parent is essential. More than essential, it is life-saving. Jonathan did not have it, and as a doctor he was unlikely to ask for it.

Returning to Spinoza's concept of conatus, in Goldstein's book I came to a paragraph about romantic love that made me sit up. In my mind I understand romantic love as any love where one's happiness depends not only on the emotions in one's own mind but those of another's, over whom basically one has no control. This puts one in a vulnerable situation. When that love is not reciprocated, the perceived rejection leads to a shattering shutting down, so much so that, in the confusion of its extreme pain, one can even desire the most irrational of all possible desires: the ceasing to be of the self (p.215). Spinoza's notion resonated with me.

An insightful psychiatrist friend of mine who is well acquainted with the details of Jonathan's suicide, also saw perceived rejection as relevant to my son's fateful decision. As he saw it from a psychological perspective, the erosion of Jonathan's sense of self-worth took place over time, resulting in depression. It was love of his children and commitment to their wellbeing that gave meaning to his life. They were his world. In fact, his love and relationship with them was the very thread that kept him functioning in the last period of his life. When that relationship appeared to him to be at risk, when in fact he thought they would be better off without him, there was nothing left in him to sustain him carrying on living. I can understand that it would have led to a shattering, a shutting down.

Had my son had some appropriate support, which would have broadened his perspective, he may have appreciated that his children at that crucial time were themselves confused and appeared not to be reciprocating his feelings. But this was likely to be a temporary phase, possibly a very short phase and, in fact, he may have misjudged their feelings. With the loss of time perspective, which, had he maintained it, would have made the distress bearable, Jonathan could not live with the extreme pain of the situation as he saw it. He appeared not to want to hear other points of view, certainly not from those close to him.

In the period following his death, I was less focused on, and did not appreciate, other multiple pressures upon my son. He was burdened financially, as he and his wife appeared to have overspent on rebuilding their house, legal costs of separation and divorce proceedings were significant and there were rumours that his hospital may be amalgamated and moved to another location, which would have affected him professionally. Even so, suicide was not the only option, and I see men in similar situations make different decisions to allow for change and hope.

Poor exam results, loss of job and loss of employment status are other vulnerabilities – building contexts found in the background of those who lethally self-injure. As my respondent Katrina wrote, it is death by a thousand cuts. One's job, one's ability to earn a living to support one's family, is a major contributor to a person's sense of self. This is true of both men and women, but traditionally it is built into men's DNA. The 45-year-old son of one of my colleagues, married with three children, lost his responsible job in a small town where his industry was shrinking. The only employment he could find was that of a labourer. He clearly felt that he had failed his family, and in his mind probably felt they would be better off without him. Another respondent reported her son's loss of job and his perceived effect on his relationship with his wife.

In the present time of the COVID-19 pandemic and the associated lockdowns in 2020 resulting in a dramatic increase in youth unemployment, data available from the National Ambulance Surveillance System for the first time shows that ambulance attendances related to self-injury between January and June in Victoria, were up 17.6 per cent compared with 2019.

Al Alvarez, in his book on suicide, *The Savage God* (1972), observed that they killed themselves because their lives, by all the standards they have built up for themselves, no longer made sense (p.87).

5

Bullying

Paul Valent, in his book Heart of Violence (2020), defines bullying as the use of physical, psychological or social strength to maliciously and intentionally intimidate, hurt and exploit another person (p.18). Being the target of bullying is another context that contributes to a person's vulnerability. In fact, the very aim of the bullying is to diminish the sense of the target's worth. The act of bullying emphasises that the victims have less or perceive that they have less power than the bully. Bullying, signifying rejection by one's peers, directly affects a young person's self-perception of being a valued, worthy member of their group. Their fledgling identity is thereby challenged.

This particularly applies to adolescents whose identity is still in a stage of development, and no matter how loving their family, the opinion of their peers is paramount. Peers provide both a sense of their value and associated belongingness.

Valent's description of bullying behaviour gives one an

understanding of what school bullying looks like in real life.

"It started with name-calling and pranks. It could escalate to grabbing of one's lunches, toys, and money. From bumping and tripping, it could develop to hitting, felling, and dunking victims' heads in water or in a toilet basin. Anal and genital touching could escalate to grabbing and forced exposure" (p.18).

Bullying is a traumatising experience for the victim, which can result in long-standing emotional and physical scars, if not death. In literature there is no more graphic depiction of the savagery and cruelty of bullying than the fate of Piggy in William Golding's Lord of the Flies.

For some vulnerable children, bullying can create an environment so threatening that they fall into significant despair and utter hopelessness. The bullying leads to a giving up, because the child feels helpless to make the bullying stop. The giving up, the surrender by the child, is associated with impaired judgement and reasoning; feeling deserted, worthless and defeated – mental and emotional features no different from those found in adults (Serani, 2019). In the mental health survey reported in Australia's Children by the Institute of Health and Welfare (2020), about 33 per cent of children aged eleven to fifteen who had been bullied said they had experienced a lot of distress caused by bullying in the previous twelve months.

Iris's anguish was obvious as she wrote about her son who committed suicide: How awful it is that some students bullied other students in the bus too and we did not think that it was him, and he told us that some teachers bullied students too and it was him. I learned this after his funeral from his friends.

Megan wrote how her sixteen-year-old son shot himself after a break up with a girl, and some online bullying she was not aware of.

Our society and school systems have become aware of the risks of bullying and have taken measures to reduce its incidence. In some ways they have succeeded in that traditional bullying, which occurs in-person or via social groups – physical or verbal – has been steadily decreasing. But cyberbullying – bullying that occurs via technology – has emerged as a major concern among parents, teachers and other professionals working with young people. Cyberbullying can cause a victim to suffer more acutely, and the child who bullies may not be reprimanded for their behaviour because of anonymity and physical distance. Megan now insists that her children turn their smartphones in to their parents at night after her middle son ended his life by suicide and she and her partner discovered that he was bullied online.

Involvement in bullying, along with other risk factors, increases the chance that a young person will lethally self-injure.

Hinduja & Patchin (2020) found that child victims of bullying or cyberbullying are nearly *twice* more likely to attempt suicide compared with their peers. The AIHW report (2020) also found that they are at higher risk of lethal self-injury. In at least one in four child suicides, bullying has been identified as an underlying narrative, or as the tipping point.

Only in a third of child suicides did the child tell someone of the bullying they were experiencing. There may be shame associated with talking about the humiliation of being a target of bullying.

Children get bullied because they are in some way different

from the stereotype of the healthy Aussie kid. Bullying is more common among children with disability, and those who identify as lesbian, gay, bisexual, trans and gender diverse.

Migrant Australians, particularly from culture-diverse and language-diverse backgrounds, are also more prone to attempting suicide as a result of bullying. Newly arrived migrants from linguistically diverse backgrounds are the most at risk. The majority are impoverished and upon arrival face imposts of economic stressors and a divide born of incidental isolation and inequalities, and many instances of the isms.

Among children who have experienced bullying, those with a major depressive disorder have a higher rate of attempting suicide. Sixty-nine per cent of these children said they experienced a lot of distress caused by bullying, compared with 29 per cent of children with no disorder.

One can find an identified target of bullying in families with many children who are under some form of stress, frequently financial. One particular child, usually perceived as less attractive either physically, mentally or emotionally, becomes the victim. That child allows the family to release some of their frustrations of not coping. I have had a father, a principled, highly religious and loving family man, confess in a counselling session that at times he found himself wanting to hit that particular daughter for no specific reason. These stressed families require support but often do not ask for it.

So, bullying, similarly to other contexts, cannot be said to directly cause suicide-related behaviour but it contributes to an individual's vulnerability. It is one thread in the complex web of vulnerabilities that put a young person at risk.

Valent, a psychiatrist and author, tells most vividly of his experience of being bullied as a child in post-war Slovakia because he was a Jewish boy – a persecuted minority group. In fact, he thought it was just part of life. He did not feel suicidal, but in his eighties, 75 years after the event, he has published a thoroughly researched book, Heart of Violence, where he grapples with the big question of what makes individuals and groups violent, what makes them commit evil deeds towards their fellow human beings. His aim was to understand the genocide of his people but also all forms of violence. The little boy who experienced bullying has not forgotten. He is now standing up to the perpetrators by trying to apply his psychological understanding.

Mental illness, such as bipolar disorder, appears in the background of a number of my respondents. Bipolar disorder has the highest rate of suicide of all psychiatric conditions and is approximately 20 to 30 times that of the general population.

Researchers estimate that between 25 per cent and 60 per cent of individuals with bipolar disorder will attempt suicide at least once in their lives, and between 4 per cent and 19 per cent will complete suicide (Miller & Black, 2020).

Just like the other conditions that contribute to vulnerability, there are other risk factors. These include male gender, living alone, divorced, no children, Caucasian, younger age (under 35 years), elderly age (over 75 years), unemployment, and a personal and family history of suicide attempts or suicide completion.

Sarah summarised the different threads that made up the web of despair from which her son chose to free himself by taking his life:

1. Mental anguish from bipolar disorder
2. Poor performance on an exam a few days earlier

3. Argument with his new wife on the night he died
4. Financial pressures.

I was fortunate that 56-year-old Kasia was willing to talk to me at length about what it was like to be in the clutches of her bipolar disorder when she was in her thirties. She has been successfully medicated by a psychiatrist she trusts over the last 20 years. She revealed how she suffered agitated depression, believing that she, a high achiever in her professional life, had failed. She thought of depression as a weakness. For her it was as if she was possessed by thoughts of her unworthiness, of how stupid she was, that she was the worst person in the world.

The worse was that these thoughts were relentless, that they controlled her. Hearing someone say, 'tomorrow is another day', struck horror in her heart. The thought of having to live another day was intolerable. Planning suicide as an exit option was a relief.

The extent to which individuals are able to control their condition with appropriate medication is a significant factor. A young woman, who had no symptoms for many years had a relapse after the death of her father and found herself needing to be hospitalised at increasingly frequent intervals, just had enough. As she put it: 'What has become of me?' What a clear expression of loss of her sense of a worthy self, of hope.

There is no evidence that reliance on a medical diagnosis and medication to predict that a specific individual will take their life is effective. This approach does not take note of the complexity of what makes up a human being. It does not tell you about the psychic pain of feeling annihilated.

6

How Well Do We Know Our Children?

As parents, we think we know our children, especially the ones to whom we are particularly close, whom we perceive to be like us. How often does one hear from a bereaved parent: 'No one saw this coming.' We know our children only up to a point, based on observation of their behaviour, but our perceptions are filtered by our own experiences and needs. One of my respondents reflected how her youngest son came from a family of high achievers, which applied to his parents and older siblings, and how she naturally expected that her youngest would follow the path of the Fergusons. But he was not a Ferguson in that sense. He chose a less travelled path. In this chapter I analyse what I now regard as my over-identification with my son, not able to see signs that were contrary to my image of what he was like.

'We did not know Jonathan was depressed', was a frequent comment from my friends and acquaintances after his death. Each time I reacted angrily and still do to that glib explanation. 'Jonathan was not depressed,' I would reply forcibly. 'He felt cornered into a situation where he saw no way out.'

In fact, as I discussed previously, the notion of suicide being the result of mental illness has been challenged, as not taking note of the whole person, as too simplistic with no evidence that it can predict lethal self-injury. One of my bereaved parents wrote that in her mind, suicide and depression are not a disease but a response to abnormal life experiences.

Yet, I now also wonder why I react so emotionally to the suggestion that he may have been depressed. I realise that my instinct and will to survive and live fully is so strong, that the notion that Jonathan could not but have that same instinct was outside my comprehension.

I have survived the murder of my young parents during the Holocaust in a little Polish town when I was five years old, leaving me with the frightening sense of being alone in the world. I have experienced numerous adjustments to new parents and schools and countries, the trauma of a beloved husband having a fatal stroke on Friday and dying the next Thursday and, of course, the suicide of my son. I am seen as a survivor. Whatever the circumstances, my friends tell me: 'You will be okay. You are a survivor.'

My thinking was that although Jonathan was going through an exceedingly difficult time, he had had a secure childhood, was much loved by many and had professional success and respect. So, his somehow ploughing through that period, painful as it was, was taken for granted by me and by all who knew him. He was my son.

One instance comes to mind. During a phone call, Jonathan let slip that he was in hospital, not as an attending physician but as a patient. He was having a blood transfusion and needed to stay in hospital for more than one day, as one transfusion was not enough. This was the time of special pressures in his divorce proceedings. Just like him, I thought, not to tell me that he was going into hospital.

I went to visit him and sat by his bed while he was having the second transfusion. Seeing him pale and weak I said: 'Jonathan, you will be alright. You will get through this. We are a family of survivors.' But he was not.

He was strong in the intellectual field. He was ambitious and intellectually most competitive as his diary, which he kept from childhood at irregular intervals well into adulthood, shows. His diary cites his place in his form (usually in the first three) and all the marks he received for every term of his schooling. He loved intellectual challenges and relished his ground-breaking research work. But emotionally, he was vulnerable.

Jonathan avoided confrontation. I cannot remember him ever expressing any anger as an adult. He functioned best, indeed flourished, in benign environments. Unlike his brother, he did not have the strong ego and fighting spirit associated with being a man in our culture. This was certainly true when applied to his personal relationships, in which he was an innocent. The note from Terry echoed my observation. She described her son as not very experienced with these [negative] emotions and that his analytical mind could not cope with them.

Terry's description of her son echoes Jonathan's reflections in his diary at age of eighteen:

"My problem has always been that I am too cerebral, in human affairs and elsewhere. I want physical and emotional contacts and feelings.

My morality is like being on a rope bridge between two peaks. Behind and in front are securities, yet I know not where to turn, and below me I see a huge chasm which may swallow me up."

Yes, Jonathan was an innocent. Yes, he did not function well in conflicted, hostile situations. In fact, he could not tolerate them. He had trouble expressing anger. In my mind this was hardly a credible explanation of why Jonathan took the unthinkable step of suicide. I did not know what was in his mind.

In exploring the varied web of vulnerabilities in a person who not only thinks of suicide as an exit option from pain but actually completes the act, I am turning to the family context in which they find themselves.

7

Family Context

An observation made by two New York psychiatrists, based on the evidence from 50 attempted suicides, startled me. They found that in a high proportion of all their cases there had been a death or loss under dramatic and often tragic circumstances, of individuals closely related to the patient, parents, siblings and friends. In 75 per cent of cases, the deaths had taken place before the patient had completed adolescence (Alvarez, p.94).

The observation made me look back on my respondents' accounts of their sons' and daughters' and, in a couple of cases, spouses' suicides. I was astounded by how often the death of a person close to the would-be-suicide in the preceding period of months or couple of years was mentioned. Megan's account stunned me with the scale of losses in her family. One son died in a car accident. Two years later her youngest son shot himself after breaking up with a girlfriend, and two years later her middle son also shot himself. Ned bemoaned the loss of his wife to suicide ten years ago. She had two sisters; one died by her own hand and the other followed thirteen years later. Although she said she would never follow them and take her own life, Ned thought her pain became too intense and she could see no other way.

Stella wrote about death in the family in the background of her daughter Jasmine, who took her life at the age of twelve. When she was nine, Jasmine experienced the suicide of her Oma the day after her Opa died of a heart attack. Her dad became depressed and the parents nearly ended up divorcing. A few months after her grandparents died, her great-grandma, whom Jasmine loved intensely, also died. Stella believes it was shortly afterwards that her daughter had her first thought of suicide. An article published in The Australian on 12 November 2020, tells of a young woman whose friend had struggled after Year 12 to find good employment, but after the loss of two close friends he was becoming involved in suicide prevention work. Then, while she was on holiday, she got a call from his mother to say that he was found too late.

To my surprise, I received a call very recently from an erstwhile student of mine with whom I had lost contact since Jonathan's suicide. Her voice sounded strained. She told me how her beautiful and very bright daughter, Chiara, had taken an overdose. Chiara had been struggling with bipolar disorder, which became worse when her beloved father, from whom her mother had been separated for a long time, died a year ago. Penelope's son, who had taken his life by jumping off a high bridge in a remote community, had lost his older friend and mentor with whom he had done some challenging and valued ecological projects.

And so it was for Jonathan. My son's adored Nana Gusta died in mid-2003, just six months before Jonathan separated and moved out of his family home. She was a strong presence in her grandsons' life. And even more, she contributed in a large part to our family's cohesiveness. She provided a focal point of belonging to the family. A photo of my sons with their arms around their Nana, both leaning into her, indicates the central role she played in our family.

Until now, I have not really thought of what his Nana's death did to Jonathan. Upon reflection, I think her death made the world a less safe place for him. Something that was always there, always fiercely protective, fiercely loyal, was gone. He would have felt more alone, more vulnerable. Even at the time of Jonathan's suicide, I thought that he would not have carried out that act of lethal self-injury during her lifetime because she would have just not tolerated it!

One can well imagine that these effects would be evident in the young suicides who lost a parent, a grandparent, a sibling – people whose existence was a sustaining part of their lives. I myself still feel the effects of my beloved adoptive father's death, 60 years after the event. I believe it would have been easier for me to meet the challenges in my life had he lived.

I also want to look at some aspects of my son's life within the immediate family context. I know little of these aspects in my respondents' families, though I imagine many may have thought about it in their private moments.

Looking at Jonathan's early life history, what stands out is a healthy pre-natal, childhood, adolescence and young adult environment in a stable, loving family. As a young woman of seventeen years, apart from wanting to go to university and complete a degree, when asked what I wanted in my life, I replied: 'I want to marry and have children'. I remember my friends being shocked to hear this from me, an academically able student having such a mundane ambition. I did marry young, and gave birth to my first son at the age of 20 and my second son at 23 years old. I was happily married and, being a young mother, quite blissful. Aside from continuing my studies, I loved my role of bringing up my boys.

And while deeply protective, I was consciously aware that my job was to nurture them to become autonomous young men. So, while dying a thousand deaths inside with worry for his safety, I encouraged Simon in his sailing a little boat on Sydney Harbour from the age of ten. We were a bushwalking and camping family and had some wonderful holidays, often with like-minded families and their children. There was a lot of laughter in our family around the big kitchen table, along with discussions about politics and current issues.

In terms of Jonathan's pre-natal experience, I was an energetic, joyous young woman and felt very well during my pregnancy. The day before he was born, I was jumping the waves at Bondi Beach in a state of exhilaration. He had a natural birth, and upon his arrival I was apparently crying out loud: 'I am so happy. I am so happy.' He was a healthy, bonny baby born to a healthy young mother. No trauma here.

The one event that would have been traumatic for Jonathan was the announcement to our sons, when they were twenty and seventeen years old, that my husband and I were separating. While Simon responded with relief as the tensions at home were affecting him, Jonathan was shocked and visibly shaken. He called his friends with the news, repeatedly emphasising that it was likely to be a temporary separation. He shut himself up in his room, making lists – of what? Plans for his life after the breakup of his family? Something none of us would ever have envisaged? He did not tell us. He did recover once we actually separated and I moved to a sunny townhouse with views of the beach, where he and Simon had a room each opening to a common balcony; a home that his friends liked to visit and was good for parties.

Thinking about my relationship with my two sons, there was a notable difference between them. Simon, as we say in the family, was born mature and with a strong streak of independence from early childhood. One could say that he was his own man. Jonathan was different.

Firstly he was genetically very much like me, the way his hair parted, the shape of his limbs, his temperament and, I would say, he identified with me and my way of looking at things. I knew how he felt or so I thought, and he knew me. For example, when Simon was deciding on a career in law, he may have sought my views but I did not think they would have had much weight, as he would work it out for himself. In contrast, when Jonathan, on finishing his medical degree, was deciding whether he should become a GP or spend many more years studying for a specialist degree, he turned to me for advice. Whereas I did not advise him directly, and just set out points for and against each choice, and would have been happy with whatever he decided, I believe his decision to go on studying was in line with what I thought he was capable of, though I may overstate my influence.

I did tend to be more protective of Jonathan. It is hard to put my finger on why this was so. I suppose that I, and even more so his grandmother, saw him as an innocent, more trusting of people, less street smart than his brother, more easily exploited. He was a gentle young man and certainly not combative, a characteristic that is often needed in life, especially by men. So there was a vulnerability in him to which I responded at both conscious and unconscious levels.

I do not believe Jonathan ever separated from me emotionally. I write this in some way critically, as boys do have to separate, in the psychological sense, from their mothers at some culturally determined point. As David Guttman pointed out in his book Reclaimed Powers (1994), before they can become men, they have to free themselves from the sense that they are their mother's little boys. At these junctures, fathers, as a strong presence in their lives, provide a secure way station on the son's psychological journey away from the mother (p.xii), and towards becoming an independent self. Unfortunately, Jonathan did not have a close relationship with his father. He was certainly not a strong presence in our son's life.

At the same time, Jonathan went confidently out into the world, studied abroad and set up his own family – all the behaviours of a responsible, adult man. Looking at families where one or both parents are survivors, closeness of family and over-identification is the norm. And the sons and daughters of these parents have gone on to establish successful lives – professionally, family-wise, and as contributors to society.

I suspect that Jonathan would have been much more aware of my deepest anxieties and fears and would have responded to them (and felt them?) more than anybody else in my life. And what has been my greatest fear? Loss of family. Everything else one can overcome, but not this. Loss of family is annihilating to me, and I believe it annihilated Jonathan.

It occurs to me that Jonathan's difficulty with being exposed to negative emotions and managing them, in fact his avoidance of situations that might trigger them, indicated a protective strategy to overwhelming arousal. Underlining the complexity of making any generalisations, this quality in him may have little connection with any traumatic experiences, mine or his. Research comparing physiological reactions of men and women to stressful and unpleasant situations has shown that men, on the whole, have greater difficulty with managing negative emotions than their female counterparts. My partner, coming from many generations of Australians with a stable background, and a solid, loving, non-traumatised family life, is also a great avoider of unpleasant and painful situations and even descriptions of pain in others.

I have written as if Jonathan had only one parent, me, and have not mentioned his father and what he may have inherited from him, indicating how much I thought of Jonathan being my son. While my older son certainly looks physically like his father and is possibly more like his paternal grandfather, there was little obvious connection between my younger son and his father – physically or intellectually. But on reflection, Jonathan inherited his father's artistic sensibility, both being outstanding photographers and perhaps more. At Jonathan's funeral, a wise old friend, a physician who knew us both very well, quietly remarked: 'Don't forget, Jonathan also had a father.' And his father was prone to depression, going through lengthy periods of what we called melancholia. I believe he took some medication but eventually it was a factor in our separation. Jonathan may have inherited a genetic predisposition to feeling low, but it certainly was not evident in any way in the young man I knew.

Jonathan's immediate family context, though not ideal, was certainly not different from many Australian families, where children adjust to the particular dynamics of their family life. Yes, there were elements that may have adversely influenced the way he functioned in the world, but again this would apply to the background of many happily functioning adults. There is not one factor that would predict the puzzle of suicide. Unmet psychological needs operate in the context of a specific environment, not only the immediate family dynamics, but of cultural forces as they interact with the family and the individuals embedded within it.

It is only recently that I have started thinking of Jonathan growing up in a family scarred by the Holocaust. Until now he was, in my eyes, a boy born in Australia into a loving and educated family with a privileged childhood and good education, holidays of camping and bushwalking, and swimming and playing cricket. But there was more, of which I was not conscious at the time.

My parents put me, their beloved four-year-old daughter, into the hands of a Polish Christian woman in the realisation that the Jewish community was standing on the verge of destruction (quote from my father's letter). By taking me out of the ghetto, they were giving me a chance to survive. It must have been an intensely painful decision but the child had to be saved.

My adoptive mother, who survived the Nazi killings by hiding but whose five siblings were all murdered, along with their children, also had the deeply entrenched belief that all that mattered were the children, her grandsons. She would say to me: 'You are not that important. All that matters is the welfare of the children, the children.' I resented it and in some ways still do, but I am at least beginning to understand that Save the Child was everything.

And I am coming back to my conviction that my son took his life in the belief that his children would be better off without him. This trans-generational belief in our family was rooted in a historical period where the murder of children was a daily occurrence.

I am gaining a glimmer of understanding of how the unfortunate intersection of Jonathan's personality and his specific context, contributed to his decision to kill himself. I also accept that going into the mind of another, whose pattern of thinking is different from one's own, is perhaps impossible.

An internationally eminent psychologist friend of mine wrote from Canada his understanding that there is *some set of psychological, physiological, genetic, and/or??? predispositional factors as to both vulnerability and the likelihood of successfully resisting the temptation to take one's life, whether with or without treatment. Hopefully, research will provide some answers but what about the ???*

8

Marriage Breakdown and Divorce

Breakdown of a major relationship such as marriage stands out as a significant red flag in the background of men who take their life. Separation and divorce proceedings appear in a number of my respondents' accounts. This also applied to Jonathan, who was going through the process of divorce and establishing a framework for contact with his children at the time of his suicide.

When children are involved in the breakdown, separation and divorce take place within the framework of the proceedings of the Family Court. Examining the processes in our society related to separation, divorce, property settlement, custodial arrangements, the role of understaffed family courts, the role of lawyers which, by their very nature, lead to adversarial attitudes, one can well appreciate the huge stresses on divorcing couples, but even more so on the children involved.

Research conducted by Martin Richard and his team in the Centre for Family Research at Cambridge University, where I spent a sabbatical, promoted the importance of divorcing couples separating and indeed insulating their role as parents with shared responsibilities for the welfare of the couple's children, from that of the often negative emotions and arguments between the divorcing couple. Sound advice but difficult to apply in high emotion divorces.

Our Family Courts offer resolution of conflict counselling and have a particular role to help families with complex needs, including those with family violence issues. Human nature being what it is, conflict resolution only succeeds in cases of amicable separation of mature and reasonable people – a desired but not frequent enough occurrence. In cases where emotions between the parents are high for many complicated reasons, as Richards found, the word reasonable does not apply.

In a thoughtful article published in The Australian on 2 January 2020, Dr David Curl, CEO of For Kids Sake, wrote how during separation and divorce, apart from experiencing grief, anger or confusion, the most important things in a parent's life are at risk: their home, financial security and relationship with their children. This applies particularly to fathers who are usually the ones who are expected to move out of the family home and immediately lose the day-to-day contact with their kids. And it is daily contact that is at the heart of bonding. Curl points out that it is a moment of enormous vulnerability for parents. It's also a moment of greatly increased risks for kids who will often find themselves for months or years to come, without the two functioning parents they have relied on.

Moreover, according to Curl, the model that family courts set for separation and divorce is of prolonged acrimonious, unaffordable separation where the escalation of potentially life-threatening conflict is inevitable. Curl argues that our society has set up support structures for other such moments of vulnerability in human life, such as guidance for gamblers, alcoholics and drug addicts, which are recognised as basically health, rather than legal, issues. But this is not so for men and women going through separation and divorce. For them there are few support mechanisms.

Anecdotal evidence suggests that in cases of acrimonious divorce, family courts have traditionally exhibited, and continue to exhibit, a gender bias in favour of the woman. In the many cases where I have talked to the parents of separating men, there is not one that does not express in the strongest terms their disappointment and anguish that the court was not fair towards their son. It could be that the perceived bias is related to views about traditional maternal child-rearing roles, which still are valid but does not take note of the changing roles of men as active co-parents.

Former WA Law Reform Commissioner Augusto Zimmermann (Arndt, 2018) explained:

> *"It is a frightening reality that here in Australia,*
> *a perfectly innocent citizen stands to lose his home,*
> *his family, his reputation, as a result of unfounded*
> *allegations. This is happening to men every day as*
> *consequent of domestic violence laws which fail to*
> *require the normal standards of proof and presump-*
> *tions of innocence. He was not talking about genuine*

cases of violent men who terribly abuse their wives and children, but law-abiding people who have lost their parental and property rights without the most basic requirements of the rule of law" (p.85).

As further evidence of gender bias in separation, divorce and custody matters, a survey of NSW magistrates found that 90 per cent agreed that Apprehended Violence Orders (AVOs) were being used as a divorce tactic. Research by Family Law Professor Patrick Parkinson and colleagues from the University of Sydney revealed that lawyers were suggesting that clients – mostly women – obtain AVOs, explaining to them that verbal and emotional abuse was enough to do the trick – to limit the father's access to their children. And the victims were the ex-husbands and fathers of the couple's children (Arndt, p.86).

An article published in The Australian on 20 April 2020 reported on a new research project to examine hundreds of intimate partner homicides that occurred between 2006 and 2018 in order to identify patterns and potential key warning signs. The project is a collaborative project of the Australian Institute of Criminology with Australia's National Research Organisation for Women's Safety. Its goal is to identify a common sequence of events, interactions and relationship dynamics in the weeks, days and moments leading up to the killing of a woman by her intimate ex- or current partner. This is an important and laudable initiative. But what about a parallel study of such events and relationship dynamics leading to suicides, especially during times of relationship breakdowns? Such research does not appear valued in our society and yet would serve as a significant contribution to understanding young men taking their lives.

Men like Jonathan find themselves fighting for their financial future, setting up arrangements for contact with their children, dealing with lawyers and preparing for Family Court hearings, while increasingly emotionally vulnerable as their world shatters. There is no doubt in my mind that the severe stresses associated with his divorce proceedings and their impact on his children and himself, need to be considered as a major factor in my son's suicide.

Apart from going through separation and divorce, the other relevant social context in Jonathan's life was his profession of medicine.

9

Suicide in the Medical Profession

Data from the 2007 National Survey of Mental Health and Wellbeing (ABS), indicated that the level of very high psychological distress and thoughts of suicide are significantly higher in doctors compared with the general population and other professionals.

An article by Sharon Verghis titled 'Wounded Healers', published in the Weekend Australian Magazine on 5 May 2018, surveyed some of the literature on suicide in the medical profession. Examination of a variety of sources identified certain patterns among doctors who took their lives. Dr Michael Myers, a New York physician, interviewed by Verghis, treats the medical profession's walking wounded on a daily basis. He knows why so many doctors choose to die. Myers observed that medicine is a victim of its own exalted status in our culture. Doctors are seen as the high priests of healing. Asking for help, admitting to weakness, burdening others is just unacceptable.

Another excellent article, by Ann McCormack (2018), echoed the view expressed by Myers, that the inherent traits in individuals who excel in the medical profession – altruism, empathy, sensitivity to the pain of others – can prove pitfalls and set them up for high rates of distress.

I was struck by how these views applied to what was happening to my son. For a start, many doctors chose to die in their medical rooms and, of course, they had access to death-causing drugs.

Loss of weight was an early indicator of extreme distress. Dissembling and carrying out their duties as expected, and relying on antidepressants, as in Jonathan's case the stimulant of appetite-suppressing tablets, was another. Verghis referred to a study by the Victorian Doctors Health Program which found that factors predisposing doctors to die by suicide included social isolation, dislocation due to losing identity as a partner and rejection by loved ones.

All these applied to Jonathan, who put his patients' care well above care of self. This was shown in the long hours, long distances travelled to be available for his patients and his patients' abundant appreciation as 'a most caring doctor', without ever a word of complaint. It was just part of his duties, which he enjoyed.

Another trait rife among doctors is perfectionism, a trait from which we, the patients, benefit. I have often said: 'I want my doctor to be a perfectionist.' I don't think that perfectionism applied to Jonathan. Research and the practice of medicine were areas in which he was confident and eminently successful. However, he would have judged himself much more harshly as a family man.

Research also shows doctors avoid accessing mental health professionals. It is something with which I have been personally struggling when I think about Jonathan. He was an intelligent man with enough insight to know that he was in great pain, in fact, despair. Why did he not seek professional help?

A recent meeting of the Council of Australian Governments Health Council agreed to remove mandatory reporting of doctors by their treating health professionals as substantial barriers exist in affected doctors accessing help. Fear of stigma and being reported to medical authorities are other barriers. These are not irrational, given studies revealing that medical professionals hold concerns over the competency of colleagues with perceived mental health disorders. I do not know if Jonathan's colleagues noticed that he was a bit flat, but if so they would have attributed it to work fatigue.

My sense is that the source of my son's distress was related to perceived personal or family failings and perceived burdensomeness. In the literature as well as in the letters I have received, personal trauma such as marriage breakdown and personal loss seem to tip the balance for a male with an at-risk profile.

On the day of Jonathan's death, I had a revealing conversation with his personal secretary, Anne, the only person to whom Jonathan had confided that he had separated from his wife and that he was in the process of divorce. That separation had happened a year prior to his suicide. She remembered that at some stage she had asked whether she could tell the secretary of their department about his divorce, since she thought that the divorce and property settlement were nearly through. Jonathan's expression changed from his usual pleasant demeanour to one of anger and anguish, and he had replied vehemently: 'No, no one is to be told'. Anne thought at the time that it was like seeing Dr Jekyll and Mr Hyde. For a moment his professional mask had dropped.

The point is that, like many physicians, Jonathan had learned to dissemble, at all times wanting to be seen and seeing himself as the healer, the one who certainly would not ask for help; as the one who coped. And, as noted, the consequence for those with high privacy thresholds is social isolation. But, tragically he was not coping. If he had been able to take a longer term perspective, if he had seen the necessity for professional help, it is unlikely he would have taken this terminal step.

Living in a remote and rural community is another social context associated with elevated rates of suicide. Personally, I was surprised with this statistic, as I have always thought of the challenges of rural life in terms of floods and fires, but also romanticised it as more tranquil, free from the speed and pressures of urban living. I was wrong.

An article published in *The Australian* on 30 September 2020 referred to a recent study which found that in the period 2010–18, suicide was about twice as common among people living in remote areas as among those living in major cities, and nearly twice as common in the bottom one-fifth socio-economic stratum of society as compared to the highest.

Tatz & Tatz's analysis on suicide in metropolitan, regional and remote areas indicated that contextual stressors relevant to the agricultural industry, relationship breakdown and Indigenous population were associated with greater risk of suicide in remote populations. Greater education, religiosity, and antidepressant use in rural populations were associated with lower suicide rates. Compared with suicides in urban localities, relationship conflict, income and work problems, and alcohol abuse disorder were significant in cases of rural suicides. The quality of available health services and possible stigma associated with help-seeking, were also highlighted as influences on rural suicide.

10

Intergenerational Transmission of Trauma

I want to explore research on the transmission of the effects of trauma suffered not only by parents but earlier generations on their descendants, and the possible links to a higher rate of suicide among them. Although I focus on research on transmission of trauma by Holocaust survivors to their offspring in this chapter, the findings are applicable to many communities in Australia.

Australia has offered a home for people from a variety of traumatised backgrounds. They include the boat people from Vietnam, people fleeing genocides in African countries, others fleeing political repression, dissidents such as from the Chinese post Tiananmen Square massacres. While we as a society focus on their economic and cultural adjustments, there is little research on the impact of their trauma on themselves and their descendants.

In Jonathan's case, his biological grandparents, whom he never knew, were murdered in the Holocaust, so that his mother was orphaned at the age of five. The concept of death, specifically violent death is embedded in the history and possibly the biology of our family. One obvious and well-established fact is that children's genetic make-up as well as the environment in which children are reared, both before and after birth, affects their development. I have often thought and written extensively about the impact on me of being told at the age of five that both my young parents had been murdered. There is no doubt that a severely traumatic event for a young child, which according to the definition of trauma, throws into question, damages or destroys any construction used by individuals to make sense of and organise reality. Mothers and fathers are supposed to be there to nurture and protect a young child. When they suddenly disappear from one's universe, the child's very existence is threatened. Childhood trauma may have long-lasting effects on how an individual reacts to adversity and stress, and there are indications that it can be transmitted to the next generation.

Until now, I have not directly considered the impact of my childhood trauma on my sons nor linked it specifically to Jonathan's suicide. I did speculate on the theme of Save the Child, which is threaded across generations of my family. It is time to explore what were the adverse as well as positive environmental and possibly genetic influences in our family that were directly or indirectly transmitted to my sons.

In the book Light from the Ashes (2001), edited by Peter

Suedfeld, to which I contributed a chapter, I wrote about myself in the third person, about little Dasia:

so sensitive to any sign of danger, who quickly learned to fear death and those who were in a position of power to hurt her and her family. She had discovered that calling yourself by your real name, asserting who you were, your religion, beliefs and ideas, were all actions fraught with danger. Survival entailed keeping quiet to fit in with the demands of threatening environments: the forest at night when the Nazis were passing through her little town; the Zbaraz ghetto when the SS were hammering at the door; having to pretend to be Stasia, an Aryan child, or later Hedda, an adopted child who must never talk about her natural parents.

Sometime in the summer of 1943, when I was five years old, a man from my father's hometown, Zbaraz, came and informed me and the Christian woman who was taking care of me that both my parents had been killed. My response is described in my book Letter from My Father:

I knew that I might get into trouble and make them angry if I cried. It was better, safer to stay silent. But now what would happen to me? Who would care for me? My parents had promised to come and fetch me after the War but now they could never come. It was so frightening. I was still a little girl. If there was nobody to hold and take care of me, I might stop being alive (p.23).

I also understood that when I fell, I had to get up by myself so that they would still want to look after me. This was essential for my survival. So my survival strategy was to be ever watchful, ever vigilant to how the grown-ups, especially people in authority, reacted to me. Any sign of displeasure was threatening and I quickly adjusted my behaviour so that they would like me, so that they would be good to me. The notion that the world was at any time a potentially dangerous place, that one had to work hard, had to continually adapt in case of a new threat emerging, was my reality.

An obvious example of how these fears have affected my behaviour is my distress when there is any argument or bad feeling or misunderstanding in the family. At the slightest sign of discord, I immediately rush to restore harmony; whatever it takes. Quite different from my late husband Sam's reaction who, coming from a big family, would not like discord but could live with it. 'Things will blow over,' he would say.

It is only now, as I am learning about the physiological and neurological effect of my early trauma, that I appreciate the source of my vigilance and anxiety. If the brain continues to perceive aspects of one's environment as dangerous, the parts of the brain involved in activating the body to fight the threat keep on prompting the release of cortisol.

Cortisol is a hormone that mobilises the body for defensive action. It activates the key survival behaviours of fight or flight or, in some situations freeze, to deal with the threat. Once the threat or traumatic incident is over, cortisol halts the alarm reaction, a brake is put on the stress response system, cortisol levels fall and the body returns to a state of balance.

But this is not necessarily so in traumatised people. Recent research by Rachel Yehuda and Amy Lehner (2018) found that Holocaust survivors have chronic higher levels of cortisol. That means that the physiologic stress response in affected people is readily recruited. The research found that the younger the survivors were during World War II, the more their stress response system was adapted to keep free cortisol in the body, ever ready for fight or flight. They are unable to find a way to put the brakes on the stress response, to switch it off. An analogy is a motorcar that is idling too high for too long. After a while, chronic low-level stress leads to wear and tear on the body, including one's immune system.

I recognised the direct relevance of this research to me. People's raised state of vigilance is exhibited, as in my case, by easily triggered perception of and anxiety about any threat to myself and my dear ones. Much of the time I am able to relax, but there is no doubt that my alarm or defensive system is easily aroused and I do suffer hypertension. I also recognise that these fears affected some of the major choices I made in life, particularly in my youth and early adulthood.

My anxiety is manageable and does not rule my life, as I was fortunate to have the significant protective factors of secure attachment to my biological parents from birth to the age of four and a half; the security, safety and care of my adoptive parents from the age of six; and, as an adult, enduring, stable and loving relationships. I was also determined, ambitious, a good student and had a great zest for life, for adventure, and was able to correct the consequences of some of the poor decisions I made.

I have exhibited the strengths found in many Holocaust survivors, referred to as post-traumatic growth. Research by eminent psychologist Peter Suedfeld (1997) has found that people whose lives have been marked by periods of danger, deprivation and challenge, show remarkable fortitude and resilience. His studies indicate that not only do they cope successfully with adversity, but exhibit self-control, rational planning and problem solving and persistence as strategies for survival. In terms of influences transmitted to one's children, they may also benefit by learning strategies for dealing with adverse circumstances

Addressing the notion of intergenerational transmission of trauma, which and how were my anxieties and my strengths transmitted to my son, if at all? How and to what extent did they contribute to his vulnerabilities?

My sons grew up with a hypervigilant mother, focused on protecting them from real or imagined dangers. Whenever we went on our family outing, be it bushwalking or just a trip to the local park or beach, I was sure to take a box of first-aid essentials, extra clothing in case the weather changed, and some snacks in case the children got hungry. My friends could rely on me to be the one who would have supplies of band-aids in her pack.

I find the following research, which is still in its infancy, disturbing yet significant. Yehuda & Lehner suggest there is now converging evidence supporting the idea that offspring are affected by parental trauma exposures occurring before their birth, and possibly even prior to their conception. Parents' stressful experiences can influence an offspring's predisposition to developing mental health disorders, including but not limited to anxiety, depression and post-traumatic stress disorder (PTSD). Experience of extreme adverse events, or more accurately the effect of that experience, can be transmitted across generations not only environmentally but also genetically via the process of epigenesis. Epigenetic refers to the process by which the effect of a traumatic experience influences the way genes work, affecting their DNA function and leaving a unique epigenetic signature on the genes. The epigenome can be affected by positive experiences, such as supportive relationships and opportunities for learning, or negative influences, such as environmental toxins or stressful life circumstances.

Yehuda & Lehner's latest results reveal that descendants of people who survived the Holocaust have different stress hormone profiles than their peers, perhaps predisposing them to anxiety disorders. Research suggests that in the absence of their own traumatic exposures, offspring of Holocaust survivors were more likely to show stress responsiveness alterations associated with PTSD. The offspring have lower levels of cortisol, a hormone which we have noted not only prepares the body for fight or flight but also helps the body return to normal, to an equilibrium, after the trauma event is over. While their parent/survivors have higher levels of cortisol – an optimal response to perceived threat – their offspring are biologically less prepared.

What is relevant is that Yehuda & Lehner's findings echo the survey of research on suicide by Rory O'Connor (2021), which found that people who made serious attempts at suicide tended to release less cortisol when put under stress. That is they were less able to activate the fight or flight response. In practice, it meant that their fighting spirit was lowered. Does this apply to successful suicides? Are they less battle-ready? The answer requires further research.

The research on the small number of studies of humans exposed to traumatic condition suggests subtle biological and health changes in their children. But Yehuda has warned that it would be premature to conclude that one generation's trauma permanently scars later generations.

What is encouraging is that researchers agree that while genetic factors exert potent influences, environmental factors have the ability to alter the genes that were inherited. Sound maternal and foetal nutrition, combined with positive social–emotional support of children through their family and community environments, will reduce the likelihood of negative epigenetic modifications (Curry, 2019).

At the other pole of sound nurturance is abuse and neglect. An online tool, released by the Australian Institute of Health and Welfare and the National Mental Health Commission, linked to the national goal of achieving zero suicide, identified child abuse and neglect as consistently the leading behavioural risk factor contributing to suicide and self-harm in Australia. Suicide accounted for about 35,000 lost years of healthy lives in 2015 alone (Aikman, 2020).

A colleague working on counselling adult survivors of child sexual abuse, of which she is one, told me of her serious attempts at taking her life as she struggled with self-hatred and loss of hope, which she linked to the sexual abuse she suffered as a teenager.

The mother of the young woman who was diagnosed as bipolar and lethally self-injured at the age of 29, related her own trauma of having been abused by her grandfather as an adolescent, well before her daughter's conception. She speculated how that may have been transmitted to her daughter.

A study by Costa and others (2018) showed that severe paternal hardship as a prisoner of war (POW) led to high mortality among sons but not daughters born after the war. Adequate maternal nutrition countered the effect of paternal POW trauma in a manner most consistent with epigenetic explanations. There are no large sample studies in human populations that examine the reversibility of paternal trauma nor the long-term impact of paternal ex-POW status on children.

The following discussion by the authors of the study

highlighted the complexity of factors involved in the explanation of the how and why of intergenerational transmission. Mechanisms for the transmission of POW trauma can be biological, cultural or psychological, or socio-economic. Parents of lower socio-economic status are less able than higher status parents to protect their children from health shocks. Poor health may lead to worse marriage matches. Cultural and psychological channels include attitudes and behaviours imparted to children and stresses during childhood from violence, family strife, emotional distance or anxiety.

Curry's (2019) discussion of the work carried out in the orphanages in Multan, Lahore, and Islamabad provide further insights. The orphanages provide shelter and health care and send kids to local schools, trying to provide the best possible support, according to University of Zurich physician and neuroscientist Ali Jawaid. But despite that, he noted, these children experience symptoms similar to PTSD, including anxiety and depression.

Jawaid set up a study within the orphanages to probe the disturbing possibility that the emotional trauma of separation from their parents also triggered subtle biological alterations – changes so lasting that the children might even pass them to their own offspring.

At this point, one can also speculate that parents separated from their children may also experience similar effects – a whole area open for study.

In animals, exposure to stress, cold or high-fat diets has been shown to trigger metabolic changes in later generations. And small studies in humans exposed to traumatic conditions – among them the children of Holocaust survivors – suggest similar subtle biological and health changes in their children.

As a case study, Jonathan had grandparents who had been murdered at a young age by people who had considered people of their ethnic, religious group as worthy of annihilation, a mother who experienced trauma at a young age and a father who was a depressive. Although we lived a comfortable, healthy, happy family life in a stable, tolerant society that offered opportunity for self-fulfilment, there was also a subterranean element of great losses, grief and hypervigilance in our family. These influences may have made Jonathan more vulnerable when exposed to a traumatic experience and limited his ability for fight or flight.

The research, in fact, suggests that under normal circumstances, the offspring may not be affected by their inherited gene modifications that control the stress response system, but during extreme stress it may be turned on. This may be an area that needs further study, as it could provide information relevant to identifying those at risk.

This is the first time I have analysed this negative aspect of the environment and possibly genetic inheritance in which my children grew up, and speculated on their influence. Speculation it is, but in my quest to understand suicide among young people, including that of my son, I need to consider both environment and genetics as possible contributing factors in their tragic action.

Rearing and protecting one's children is at the centre of most parents' lives, but certainly so of survivors of historical traumas, such as genocide, for whom the urge to build new families appears biologically overwhelming. The family. The family is all. Thus the thought that my own trauma may have contributed environmentally or genetically to my son's vulnerability and his inability to live with and manage what he perceived as threat to his family is most confronting. We parents of young suicides keep asking what could we have done to make them stay, and the possibility that things over which we had no control may have adversely affected our children is most troubling.

Presently there are discussions about the impact of historical events such as colonisation, slavery and displacement trauma in many cultures, including First Nations and Native American communities, African Americans, Australian Aboriginals and New Zealand Maoris, as well as in societies exposed to genocide, ethnic cleansing or war, such as Cambodians, Armenians, Rwandans and communities in the former Yugoslavia. This is an area that requires much more research generally, but specifically in the Australian context with our high percentage of refugees and other migrants from potentially traumatic social environments.

While it is not possible to attribute intergenerational effects in humans to a single set of biological or other determinants at this time, it is another part of the puzzle in understanding the complex factors that are associated with a healthy young person taking their life.

11

Low Tolerance for Negative Emotions

Each act of suicide is directly related to the interaction of two things: the specific contexts and conditions that contribute to their vulnerability, which include family dynamics and social contexts; and the temperament or personality of the individual suicide. Thomas Joiner's book Why People Die by Suicide (2007), explores the specific characteristics of people who actually carry out a successful suicide, or what Joiner calls lethal self-injury.

Literature on suicide supports the view that people desire to stop living when two fundamental needs are frustrated to the point of extinction: the need to connect or belong to others; and the need to feel effective or influence others versus perceived burdensomeness. The consequence of these unmet needs is hopelessness about being a burden to others and a sense that one's life is worthless. These consequences manifest themselves intense psychic pain or in Spinoza's words, "a shattering, a shutting down."

There were multiple stressors in Jonathan's life in the period preceding his suicide. The primary factor of breakdown of his marriage and his anguish and fear of losing his close relationship with his beloved children was overwhelming. Added to it were loss of home, social isolation, financial and professional concerns. This pile-up of high stress circumstances and their effect on his psyche would put any person at risk, but none of them singly or together necessarily predict taking the action to kill oneself.

I have written in earlier chapters that my son's physiological and or psychological make-up made it difficult for him to manage negative emotions. He functioned extremely well in benign situations, but although he did what was required, he was not good at managing situations that involved the complexities of the nastier side of human behaviour, such as envy, unscrupulousness and injustice.

I am coming to understand that a person like Jonathan who has a low tolerance for negative emotions or, as previously quoted, Terry's son, who was not very experienced with these [negative] emotions and that his analytical mind could not cope with them, just cannot physiologically or neurologically endure extreme emotional pain. They do not have that extra protection from the desire to leave the painful situation, to die.

Paradoxically, as a doctor, a cardiologist, Jonathan had many experiences of dealing with pain, disease and death, but when I occasionally questioned him on how he could bear so much pain in his daily professional life, he would reply that he saw these situations as problems to be solved rather than pain to be endured. There were situations when the death of a patient may have affected him deeply, but here again, if it did, he did not show it.

In Marsha Linehan's view (1993), one can acquire the ability to manage negative environments, but fundamentally, they are certainly part of one's genetic make-up. People with low tolerance for negative emotions – I prefer this term to Linehan's biological deficits – tend to construct protective mechanisms in their personal and professional lives to reduce exposure to emotions they cannot handle. Again, Jonathan constructed his professional life in such a way as to reduce combative, potentially stressful environments. He chose to work in the more benign environment of a smaller hospital rather than the more political and potentially more prestigious environment of a big public hospital. In his personal life, especially in the period of separation and marriage breakdown, he felt that he had neither any choices nor experience. Unable to change the situation, he took action in the area where he had sovereignty and power – his decision whether to continue to live or not.

Having written the above something suddenly strikes me. Jonathan, like all of us, did experience negative emotions but had difficulty expressing them verbally or in his actions. A passage from his diary comes to mind with great clarity:

> *"I came back from a week's skiing … I seized my guitar and played with a mad fury and passion, to extract sound and fury and meaning. I was fused with it. I did not want beautiful or melodic sounds; I wanted power and emotion – flamenco, not classical form. I wanted love and hate and sorrow and anger."*

Hate and sorrow and anger – all powerful negative emotions that my son felt deeply but expressed only or mainly through music.

Although he gave up playing the guitar as long fingernails necessary for guitar playing and practising medicine did not go together, he was still able to play at times and play well. But somehow in the last years of his marriage and his extensive travels to the various locations where he worked as a public hospital and private practice physician, there was no occasion when we heard him play. Then, one day when I was visiting his and his wife's new modern house with its lovely finishes, I asked about the guitar and Jonathan replied: 'There is no room for it in the house, so I sold it'. I remember being stunned and quite distraught. No room for the guitar, the guitar he loved? Hard to fathom. But he allowed himself to take this step and close off the conduit to an authentic part of himself – a connection to the emotions he craved to express. An enormous shutting down of an essential part of his self! In retrospect, this was a red flag. I felt uncomfortable about it at the time, but did not apprehend its significance.

I know from personal experience that one's capacity to suffer the most agonising emotional pain is a factor in survival. In writing this sentence, I realise there was more to my survival of extreme emotional pain following my son's suicide. I had a powerful motive to live. Victor Frankl, in his seminal book The Unheard Cry for Meaning (1978), developed the theory that a basic human need is to find meaning in one's life. In his study of how concentration camp survivors coped with the most inhuman, beyond horror conditions, he found that a key factor in those who survived was their connection to another human being, either present or a distant loved one, for whom they wanted to live. The hope to see them, to reconnect with them, enabled them to carry on their wretched existence.

Frankl also postulated that even when confronted with a hopeless situation as its helpless victim, what counts and matters is to bear witness to the uniquely human potential at its best, which is to transform a tragedy into a personal triumph, to turn one's predicament into an achievement (p.43). In my case, after my son's suicide, I had another son and five grandchildren for whom I was committed to do just that, to bear witness, to model survival in extremis. I wanted, above all, for them not to ever think of suicide as an option in difficult situations.

For Jonathan, the perceived disconnect with his children took away the paramount meaning of his life. Its loss accounted for his hopelessness. I have no doubt that if he had, in any way, felt that his life would enhance his children's welfare and happiness, he would have born any pain, any discomfort.

Going back to Linehan's point that one can acquire adaptive ways of tolerating and handling negative emotions, I wonder about all the young men who went off to fight in World War I, many thinking of it as an adventure and a way to serve their country, only to finish off in years of degrading conditions of life and death in the trenches. Many would have been similar to my son and the other young men in my survey on low tolerance for negative emotions, and yet they endured, some better than others. And here again, it is likely that those who kept up correspondence with their sweethearts, with their mothers and fathers, their siblings and who maintained a belief that they were fighting for the future of their country, would have handled the deprivations more effectively. For them, there was meaning in their lives.

My late husband, who enlisted in the Australian army at the

age of eighteen to fight the Japanese, told me of the training the new recruits received before being sent overseas for active duty. While he came from a protected middle-class family that at times had experienced poverty, he was a most beloved and doted on little boy in a three-generation family. So what followed was a shock to him. Part of the young recruits' training was for them to hold a bayonet and run towards an artificial target into which to thrust the bayonet while shouting: 'Kill. Kill.' It is impossible for me to judge whether the training hardened my husband, though I think he already had a combative nature.

My son neither had this nature or training, and nor did the other young men who lethally self-injured.

12

High Levels of Privacy

The consistent anguish from parents and those close to a suicide is: No one saw it coming. Why did they not talk to us? Why did they not share their feelings of despair? Why did they not ask for help? Joy's note echoed that cry: "I cannot understand why he did not come to us as we were there for him? We believed he would talk when he was ready."

The unfortunate answer is that those who are successful suicides do not want to be stopped in their decision. But there may be other explanations.

Liz, who lost two sons through suicide, wrote how her boys were secretive, but they also felt anxiety to a huge degree. "I feel they were ashamed of their anxiety and kept it secret until it was unbearable. Penelope lamented that at no stage did he reveal the true depth of his despair. "Our sons did not reveal the utter anguish that one assumes they felt in making the suicide decision."

In Jonathan's case, he did not mention his separation and imminent divorce to his colleagues with whom he worked closely on a daily basis, both in the hospital setting and in his private practice. He had confided only in his secretary. I was shocked to hear after the funeral that nobody knew about the challenges he was facing. What stopped him from sharing this big thing in his life?

Jonathan, a doctor, might well have been afraid of being labelled and judged for what he may have seen as a stigma – something of which he was ashamed? Did he fear that his situation would be misunderstood?

A high level of privacy is, as discussed, an aspect of being a doctor, the helper, with total focus on the needs of the patient. When we visit a doctor, we are not interested in their private life and this seems to carry over to their social life, where friends often see the doctor part rather than other parts of their medical friend's personality.

In fact, on the morning on which he took his life, Jonathan's car was parked in the hospital car park in an unusual and awkward position, as if parked in a hurry. One of Jonathan's closest colleagues, with whom he was working on a project, noticed it and was surprised as Jonathan did not usually come to the hospital on weekends. But he was pleased, as he wanted to discuss some research issues with him. The door to the suite where Jonathan's rooms were located was closed, so his colleague decided not to interrupt him and postponed the meeting. Later he lamented: "If I had only known that Jonathan was going through separation and divorce, I would have gone in and if necessary broken the door down." He understood the anguish of the situation as someone in his family had gone through a similar experience. But, alas, he did not know.

A high privacy threshold was a feature of Jonathan's personality from childhood. Not being open with your emotions is also part of being a male in our culture. This is something I explore in Chapter 18, 'What Is it About Men?'

It is only now that I have become aware of some relevant research on the relationship between high threshold of privacy and suicide.

Individuals who experience a medically severe suicide attempt have been found to be very similar to individuals who complete suicide. On this basis, a significant study in Israel by Yossi Levi-Belz investigated the role of mental pain – what we have referred to as psychache – and communication difficulties in a group who had experienced a medically severe suicide attempt that required hospitalisation. They were compared with a group who made a medically non-serious suicide attempt; a group of psychiatric patients who had no history of suicidal behaviour; and healthy controls (no psychiatric or suicide background).

The specific communication dimension studied was self-disclosure, defined as the process of communication by which one person reveals information about themselves to another. Whereas people like Jonathan and generally men as such may be quite articulate about sharing their views on impersonal matters, they may be very limited in disclosing feelings, especially negative ones, such as distress and straight-out unhappiness. I had never considered that unwillingness to be open about one's feelings as a communication difficulty, but this is how the author of this study and related ones defined it. And this difficulty is, of course, what we mean when we talk about high privacy threshold.

The study assessed aspects of mental pain (for example, hopelessness), facets of communication difficulties (such as self-disclosure), as well as socio-demographic and clinical characteristics in the four groups. Individuals in the medically severe suicide attempts had significantly higher communication difficulties than those in the other three groups. Difficulty with self-disclosure put them at high risk of committing a medically serious suicide attempt. The study concluded that co-existence of unbearable mental pain with difficulties in communication significantly enhances the risk for lethal forms of suicidal behaviour.

Another study (Levi and others, 2008) also concluded that problems with sharing of feelings with others is an important risk factor for lethal or near-lethal suicide, over and above the contribution of mental pain. So, it makes sense that individuals with intense psychache who cannot signal their pain to others are at high risk of taking their lives.

Having written the above, I came across a quite different interpretation of why would-be-suicides avoid sharing their distress and thoughts. To a colleague of mine who made three serious attempts to jump off The Gap, a popular suicide spot in Sydney, the notion of taking her life was an insurance policy, an exit plan for her unbearable searing despair. Having the exit plan taken away from her would have thrown her into an increased cycle of psychic pain. For her it was not a communication difficulty but clinging to the one and only hope she had to liberate herself from pain that motivated her secrecy about her intentions.

It must be emphasised that it is not a high level of privacy

– which is a characteristic of the personality of many people, more often men – that is a risk factor in itself, but it becomes one when combined with thwarted belongingness, a sense of being worthless and a burden to one's loved ones, with intense mental pain.

Jonathan tended not to self-disclose, was a male under stress and a doctor, both categories over-represented in successful suicides.

13

The Ability to Complete the Act of Suicide

Suicide is an extreme and difficult form of action. Camus' statement, quoted previously, puts it well: "The body's judgment is as good as that of the mind's, and the body shrinks from annihilation" (Camus, p.6).

No matter how meaningless one's life is, no matter how one wants to end the pain of one's existence, only a very strong person can actually carry out the act of lethal self-injury. To do so, one needs to overcome the most powerful instinct of nature, that of self-preservation. Many people who fervently desire death attempt suicide, some many times but they cannot and do not complete the action. They stop in the final moments of the act.

In Joiner's view, the only ones who are capable of that lethal act have extraordinary courage and competence, specifically regarding suicide. They may need to work up to the act of death by repeatedly exposing themselves to painful or provocative situations, thus lowering their resistance to lethal self-injury. Penelope wondered whether her son, who jumped off a very high bridge, had secretly practised it before the actual act. She described him as a daredevil, so it would not have been too hard for him. Joiner gives many examples of, and quotes research on, how people who eventually completed the act of suicide had a history of suicide attempts or experienced other painful situations. Would-be suicides become fearless by doing things that most people would be too fearful to contemplate or attempt. For example, one may practise jumping over a bridge by initially just putting one foot over the edge of the rail, then on another occasion taking one risky step further until they actually jump to death.

According to this view, repeated smaller acts of self-injury are necessary for the evolving competence and fearlessness involved in serious suicide behaviour to occur. Of course, fearlessness and competence may be necessary in suicide behaviour but by themselves do not lead to suicide. I heard an interview on the radio with a young woman who since childhood engaged in dangerous, risky acts such as jumping off the roof of her family house as a nine year old, running a marathon along the Great Wall of China and then going on to becoming a boxer. I imagine circus artists practise death-defying acts as part of their performance and way of earning a living. It may be that, if the other two key factors of a sense of one's worthlessness and burdensomeness as well as loss of connection were present, they would have the courage and competence to inflict serious damage to themselves.

When I first heard Joiner interviewed on the radio, he emphasised that successful suicides were those who had a high degree of physical courage. I was driving a car at the time and in astonishment, I pulled over and listened to the rest of the interview. Physical courage was one of Jonathan's strongest characteristics, and he certainly had experience in doing what others may call risky activities that to him were just challenging and thrilling. He was a daredevil is a phrase that also recurs in my respondents' accounts.

In my little self-published book Letter to My Son, I described the many examples of Jonathan's daredevilry that required me, his mother, having nerves of steel to observe or listen to others tell me about his adventures and thrills. I referred to him being a fearless climber, up trees, rock ledges and anything else climbable. I was unable to leave him at children's parties under the supervision of the hostess or a friend, as they considered him too wild. While other children may have been playing on the swings or slippery dips, Jonathan was likely to be found climbing the fence or the tallest tree. His behaviour was too much for my friends to handle.

In terms of practising dangerous situations, my son certainly did a lot of that as a child. As an adult he climbed to the base camp on Mount Everest.

These acts of fearlessness were in my mind part of his vitality and curiosity and, in fact, would have taken him into untrodden paths intellectually. How difficult it is now to find that these strengths may have facilitated his suicide.

To my surprise, I came across an observation that daredevils are often injured, so they habituate to injury and thereby may be more prone to self-injury. When thinking about Jonathan, my first thought is that Jonathan may have been a daredevil, but he was also very agile and had few accidents. Rather, I would say that his adventurous behaviour allowed him to practise and develop courage and competence.

Apart from the view that habituation to pain is involved in suicide behaviour, research also indicates suicidal persons have a higher tolerance for pain and appraise the pain as less intense than those who are classified as non-suicidal. Jonathan certainly exhibited a high pain threshold from childhood. At times, this threshold resulted in him not getting appropriate and timely medical help. Two instances come to mind. On picking up seven-year-old Jonathan from school, I noticed that his arm was hanging at an awkward angle and that he was rather pale. I rushed him to a nearby surgery and the doctor immediately diagnosed a badly broken arm. It was not clear how it had happened, but apparently it was hours before I came. Nobody at school had noticed what appeared to me quite obvious, and Jonathan had not approached a teacher to tell about the pain. He just bore it quietly.

On another occasion, believing that Jonathan was playing outside with the neighbour's children, I heard a sound coming from Jonathan's room and to my surprise found him lying in his bed. He did not look well. He had fallen and hit his head hard and, not feeling good, had come to his room and lay there quietly. Again we rushed him to the doctor who diagnosed mild concussion. Bearing pain seemed natural to him. In my view, he did not purposely practise bearing pain. Rather, I think he was simply one of these people who are born with a high pain threshold.

In Chapter 9 I wrote about the higher rate of suicides found in the medical professions as compared with the general population, and discussed aspects of the profession that may account for this statistic. Within the framework of this chapter, physicians become familiar with the consequence of pain, violence and injury, and they gain specialised knowledge about lethal agents, dosing and methods of death. Karl Menninger (1936), a physician, observed that: "We physicians, familiar from our daily experience with these unlovely sights, often forget that for most persons these barriers imposed by taboos are quite high" (p.203).

Physicians are in a unique position to develop competence and capability regarding suicide. That applied to my son. In his medical practice, injecting oneself at times or one's patients would have been an everyday common occurrence. He had the knowledge and the means. The actual act was a familiar part of his repertoire, and he knew that an intravenous injection with potassium chloride would cause immediate cardiac arrest, so that there would be no pain.

I have some understanding of Jonathan's behaviour and thinking, because he may have inherited some of my genes related to physical courage and high pain threshold. I am relatively fearless, as for example when on a trek in the Himalayas, I would be the first in our group to offer to walk across a swinging threadbare bridge strung over an abyss. I have a history of jumping from the top of a garage as a child, swinging on gates and crushing my hand, climbing tall trees into adulthood and parasailing in my seventies. I have not practised my fearless acts, I do not wish in any way to injure myself. I just get a thrill doing them. I also tend to be single-minded.

I imagine that if I felt worthless, that I was a burden to my loved ones, that I had lost my connections to what is central to my life – my children and grandchildren – then I also would have the ability to lethally self-injure. But, of course, thinking about it is not doing it. The courage required to complete that action is enormous.

14

Thwarted Sense of Belonging

The need to belong is a fundamental human need. Connection to another specific human being is the basis of one's sense of security. In human development, our initial affiliation is within our family of origin – our parents or parental figures, our siblings, grandparents and extended family. Most adults go on to form their own family of whatever configuration in which secure attachment is fundamental. In Western cultures, one is expected to become less dependent, emotionally and financially on one's parents, something that parents often experience as the empty nest syndrome. The adult children fly off to form their own family unit, which then comes to satisfy their need for belongingness. Within this new unit, the bond between the spouses or partners forms the foundation on which the family can grow and thrive.

According to Joiner, belonging involves a combination of frequent interaction plus persistent caring (p.96). For this bedrock need to be satisfied, the interactions must be frequent and positive, such as one finds in what is commonly called a good marriage or relationship.

The unmet need to belong is one of the two major contributors to the desire for death. Thwarted belonging can be thought of as the psychological equivalent of deprivation of oxygen.

As discussed earlier, a recently ruptured relationship is in the background of most of the reports of my respondents. Denise wrote so eloquently about her son: "I think this was the failing sense of belonging and the loss of connection to everyone he knew and loved."

Reflecting on my son, I can see an inherent risk in the way his family unit functioned. Jonathan and his wife got engaged only a very short time after meeting each other and went on to have children within a year of marriage. They had little time to become a couple. It was evident that their primary commitment was to their children rather than to each other. In other words, what bonded them was their mutual commitment to raise their children. They were partners in their task of parenting. Their thoughts, actions and talk were ever focused on the children. My son's need to belong was satisfied by his role as a co-parent, a father.

Although they had opportunities to get away as a couple and have a holiday away from the children, to just enjoy each other, to nurture their bond, they never did so in the twelve years of their marriage. There are marriages like that that function well for many years but there is, in the long term, an inherent risk in not satisfying the couple's need for belongingness.

In psychological research, a healthy functioning model of

family postulates that the strength of the bond of the couple is paramount, and that it is from this base that they commit to their role as parents. After all, our task as parents is to help our children develop into autonomous individuals, who as young adults separate from their families of origin and go on to grow their own families. The couple's commitment to each other and mutual connectedness continues. The continuing bond also provides a model of a satisfying relationship for our children. I know that at the time of his marriage, Jonathan was totally committed to a good, lasting marriage that would form the basis of a family and satisfy his deepest needs for connection. He had suffered the consequences of marriage breakdown by his parents, this was not going to happen to him, nor his children. I witnessed the many ways he adapted to whatever he saw as necessary in order to make the marriage work. Divorce for him would not have been envisaged, even at the cost of unmet needs.

When the marriage broke down, all his energy, passion, appetite and ambition were aborted. Being the highly principled man he was, Jonathan would have taken a disproportionate responsibility for the marriage not working. What is more, the dynamics of his marital relationship were such that he would have felt that whatever was wrong was due to his own failings.

Once Jonathan's marriage ruptured, he was determined to form a new unit to which he would be committed – that of himself and his children. His wife no doubt felt the same. It would be this new smaller unit that would fill his need for deep connectedness. When that belongingness was thwarted or appeared to him to have failed, he had nothing. Yes, he was loved by me, his mother, who had happily remarried and his brother, who was in his own stable marriage, but he would have felt we were in our own units of connectedness while his primary connection was no longer there.

In the context of family connection, Alvarez wrote about the effects of industrialisation and urbanisation on family structures and how the old pattern of family life – grandparents, parents and children living under one roof – protected each member from self-destruction. Joiner also cited evidence that having large numbers of children protects against suicide (p.125).

Some of the examples of failed belongingness found in suicide notes include: "I haven't the love I want so bad there is nothing left for me; I have this empty feeling inside me that is killing me; I just cannot live without you. I might as well be dead."

What is more, the pain of thwarted belongingness is perceived by the body as physical pain. After all, it is a threat to one's existence.

It is saddening for me and the other parents who wrote to me, that our children did not reach out to us; that our love, the parent–child bond, was not enough to satisfy their need to belong. Nor did they think of what it would do to us. They were in their own world.

There are some parallels between Jonathan's experience and mine, but I did not lose my children. I had married very young, had my first baby within nine and a half months, so I was from the beginning more of a mother than a wife. Although I believed I performed the functions of a wife well enough, the children were my primary commitment. We divorced when both our sons had finished their schooling. But it was me with whom our young adult sons continued to live and enjoy being a family. My ex-husband soon found a new relationship and so did I.

Of course, there are other sources of belongingness within

a community, such as sports clubs, hobby groups, groupings around one's religious affiliation and a vast variety of charity organisations. Involvement and participation in them allows one to develop a sense of affiliation not just with the association but also with its individual members.

As an example, my partner is a passionate supporter of AFL, an Australian football game. He attends matches, sits with his mates year after year, and along with his fellow enthusiasts, is exhilarated when his team wins and downcast when they lose. He likes to wear the red and white colours of his team and no matter where he is, if there is another supporter of his team, they will recognise each other and immediately bond. In his world of sports team affiliation there is always a person who turns round when one enters, who wants to talk to you, who acknowledges you as a member of his community. You belong.

A powerful example of the link between suicide and thwarted belongingness is the experience of young Aborigines and Torres Strait Islanders, who take their lives at significantly higher rates than the rest of the Australian population. While the national suicide rate is now 12.6 per 100,000 of the population, for Aborigines and Torres Strait Islanders it is at the 24 per 100,000 level (Tatz & Tatz , p.86).

Aboriginal people of Australia have suffered multiple losses of connections (Hari, 2018): Loss of land, of life, of kin, of children, language, traditional culture and ritual (often forbidden by statute), of freedom of movement, of a hunter-gathering lifestyle. They have experienced forcible relocation, loss of choice of living space (pp.256–7).
According to Tatz & Tatz, their suicide rate is a rational response to overwhelming thwarted connections that have underpinned their lives.

15

Perceived Burdensomeness

Seeing oneself as a burden, a belief that those close to one would be better off without one, is the second bedrock factor in developing a desire for lethal self-injury. My councillor at the Bereavement Care Centre, which I attended for six months after Jonathan's death, observed that Jonathan 'died out of love for his children'. Nearly all the notes I received from my respondents refer to their loved sons perceiving themselves as being a burden.

Perceived burdensomeness arises from thinking of oneself as ineffective, as a failure. Believing that one is ineffective to a degree that those close to you are burdened is among the strongest sources of all for the desire for death. It arises out of altruism, a desire to make others better off, to remove the perceived burden. Perceiving that one is of no value to one's loved ones, that one is a burden to them is a stronger predictor of suicide than a sense of hopelessness and emotional pain.

It is interesting that four centuries years ago Spinoza wrote about the effects of a person seeing themselves as ineffective and how this leads to a shattering, a shutting down. As cited earlier, Spinoza postulated that to experience a decrease in one's power to persist, to feel one's self-diminishing, contracting out of the world is pain. His deep understanding came from philosophy, well before our empirical studies of psychology and sociology.

In the first century, the Roman statesman and philosopher Cicero wrote: "When a man's circumstances contain a preponderance of things in accordance with nature, it is appropriate for him to remain alive; when he possesses or sees in prospect a majority of the contrary things, it is appropriate for him to depart from life" (Tatz & Tatz, p.36).

Cicero took the Stoic view that while life must be suffered, and reason and virtue guide the individual, suicide delivered an acceptable end to pain and dotage, an end without stigma or shame once all reasoning and considerations had been evaluated.

One factor that affects one's sense of effectiveness, particularly in young men, is their ability to earn a living, be a breadwinner. In a number of notes I received, my respondents refer to financial worries, loss of job, loss of status and poor exam results in the background of their children who took their lives. Joiner confirms that financial hardship constitutes a risk factor for suicide. Indeed, life insurance may figure in the thinking of would-be-suicides, in the sense that they would calculate their loved ones would be financially better off as a result of their lethal self-injury.

This may well have also applied to my son. Jonathan was financially under severe pressure. My husband, an accountant, calculated that he would have had to earn two and a half times as much as he earned – and it was quite a substantial amount based on his qualifications and holding down a private and public practice – to cover the cost of the rebuilding of his family house, followed by costs of divorce settlement and setting up two households. He may have considered that his life insurance would ease the financial pressures on his family.

Thinking of Jonathan as ineffective appears quite illogical. In fact the opposite would be true. He had been successful in nearly all aspects of his life: an outstanding scholastic record at school and at university, followed by a brilliant medical career. He was loved by his family, friends and colleagues. He was good looking, talented in music and had a highly developed sense of aesthetics.

The following extract from one of the eulogies at Jonathan's funeral by one of the senior physicians at his hospital, tells of Jonathan's achievements: "In a tragically shortened career, Jonathan made an internationally recognised contribution to the treatment of patients with heart disease."

How could this gentle, and in personal relationships innocent man, ever ask: 'Mum, am I really so worthless?'

Terry wrote that her 34-year-old son did not exhibit any mental health issues whatsoever. He was a very successful electrical engineer, who was extremely loyal and highly regarded in his workplace and in his personal life. Everything he did he achieved highest acclaim for. His mother considers the breakup of his relationship the contributing factor to her son's suicide. Like Jonathan, his analytical mind could not cope with the accompanying confused emotions.

The observation that those who die by suicide experience isolation and withdrawal before their death is among the clearest in all research literature on suicide. In a study of psychiatrists' reports on patients who died by suicide, three variables stood out in the months preceding the suicide: social isolation, feeling a burden on others and not asking for help (Joiner, p.123).

16

Suicidal Ideation

Suicidal ideation refers to having thoughts, fantasies and wishes about ending one's life. I can only guess at what moment it occurred to my son that suicide was the best option for himself and likely the best for his children, but once the idea occurred to him as a means of removing himself from his anguish, he would have thought about it and in a sense mentally rehearsed the action. This is what we naturally do in most challenging or unfamiliar situations, be it a job interview or meeting a new date or confronting a potentially challenging activity or encounter.

Research refers to it as cognitive sensitisation. In terms of suicide, cognitive sensitisation occurs when one starts thinking of ending one's life as a viable solution to an unbearable situation, as one experiences it, and subsequently suicide-related images and behaviours become more accessible and active. What is to most of us unthinkable becomes thinkable. Mental practice may facilitate suicide completion, especially among those attempting it for the first time (Joiner, p.81).

The duration and intensity of suicidal ideation vary. Today, as I am focusing on the period prior to Jonathan's suicide, I get a sudden flashback to the evening when the thought of suicide may have occurred to my son. One of his children was receiving a number of prizes at their school's annual prize-giving evening. As Jonathan was at work and would arrive just before the beginning of the ceremony, he asked me to get there early to secure a front row seat so that he could take photographs of the occasion of his pride and joy. He was a keen photographer. He called during the day to remind me of the importance of being early as the hall would fill up quickly. I did not need reminding and noted his anxiety around the evening. Dutifully, I arrived an hour early, was one of the first in the auditorium and secured front seats. On arrival, Jonathan was pleased with the seat and set up his elaborate camera equipment. We both glowed with pride and joy on seeing his child receive multiple awards, with Jonathan taking numerous shots.

At the end of the ceremony, Jonathan rushed up to his child to offer his congratulations and a big hug, with me lagging behind, when the prize winner turned away from us, as if we were complete strangers, as if we were not there, and stalked off. What was the reason for that strange behaviour? It could have been the child's embarrassment at the over-attention they were getting in front of their schoolmates. In retrospect I think now of the poor confused children torn in different directions by the parental conflict in which they found themselves, and deciding that showing attention to their father would displease their mother. But both Jonathan and I interpreted that moment as rejection.

It was late evening when we left and walked to the car. We walked slowly, side by side, in silence. Jonathan was withdrawn, deeply inside himself. Normally, I can be relied on to say something positive, to chat about the ceremony, always trying to cheer up my loved ones, but on this occasion there was nothing I could say. I suppose I did not want to intrude into his thoughts and feelings. He was alone. All I could do was feel his humiliation and his aloneness. When Jonathan dropped me off home, I knew that something dark had happened. I could not name it, but I knew it.

In 1890, William James, the great American philosopher and psychologist wrote that when a person is absolutely unnoticed in society, when one is cut dead as if one were nonexistent, in this case by those who most mattered, a kind of rage and impotent despair would before long well up in us, from which the cruellest bodily torture would be a relief. Is that what my son was feeling?

That could well have been the moment when the desire to die, the desire to escape the pain, was planted in my son's mind. It may have been the moment when he entered the Sealed Box of Suicide, as Tatz & Tatz conceived it. I have also come across the notion that once suicide ideation takes hold in one's mind it forms a closed circle, which is hard to access for those outside, no matter how close and loving they are. Alvarez, a failed suicide, wrote: "I had entered the closed world of suicide and my life was being lived for me by forces I couldn't control" (p.227).

Did this apply to my son? To the other young men and women who chose not to live? It is impossible to know, but somehow intuitively it makes sense.

Suicidal ideation, however, does not in itself predict suicide. A landmark study by the University of New South Wales in

2019 revealed that the majority – 60 per cent – of people who died by suicide had denied expressing suicidal thoughts when questioned by their physician in the weeks and months prior to their death (Tatz & Tatz, p.51). Analysis of the results showed that only 1.7 per cent of people with suicidal ideas died by suicide. Therefore, being preoccupied with thoughts and even planning the logistics may not be a crucial test of actually carrying out the act.

17

Planning and Preparing for the Act

Albert Camus' empathetic statement that an act like this is prepared within the silence of the heart resonates with me. Boris Pasternak's comment shows great compassion:

> *"We have no conception of the inner torture that precedes suicide. Though we, the bereaved and social scientists and psychiatrists, focus on what appear immediate circumstances, we know little of the long, slow, hidden processes that lead up to it. These processes are at least as complex and difficult as those by which he continues to live" (1959, p.91).*

But one keeps on trying to understand.

Courage and competence to overcome the powerful and natural instinct for self-preservation are necessary for those who successfully complete the act of suicide. Alongside of competence, one needs to have an overpowering desire to no longer live.

Two categories of suicidal symptoms have been identified in the research literature: resolved plans and preparations and suicidal desire and ideation – that is, thinking about and wanting to die. The resolved plans and preparations are significantly related to serious suicide behaviour (Joiner).

Carol was able to identify her son's planning the end of his life, as he still lived at home. She was able to reflect on what she observed but understood only in hindsight. During the last week, her 24-year-old son was binge drinking and smoking heavily; made up with a friend with whom he had had a falling out; bought tickets to travel to Melbourne with his girlfriend but took a travel insurance on it; said goodbye to various people; and bought a pair of very expensive jeans which he in fact used to hang himself (Woolley, p.19).

As I reflect on the days and weeks preceding Jonathan's suicide on Saturday 8 January 2005, I can clearly identify the steps he took in the planning phase. I do not know if he could have been stopped at this stage, but he was on his way.

As mentioned in an earlier chapter, Jonathan took his children to a holiday resort in Queensland in the last week of December. On return he thanked me for suggesting that particular resort, telling me that the time with his children was 'wonderful, wonderful'.

The 7th of December, one month prior to his death, was the first day of the Jewish holiday of Chanukah, at which presents are exchanged, similar to Christmas time. At Jonathan's request

I prepared the traditional meal for him and the children. He arrived with a bundle of carefully wrapped gifts for his children that were unusually generous for this type of occasion. They included a clarinet for his musical son. I had understood the instrument was what Jonathan had intended to give his son the following May, on the occasion of his bar mitzvah. It was much too expensive a gift for Chanukah, 'over the top' as I told him. I remember feeling slightly uneasy about it. Jonathan must have already considered the possibility that he would not be there for his son's life-marking occasion.

I remember Jonathan's preparation for the holiday he had with his children. He took care of every detail of how to make every aspect fun for them – a holiday to remember. And on return they did think it was great. Perhaps he was already thinking that it was their last? Perhaps it was part of his planning?

There was only a week between Jonathan and his children returning from their holiday and his suicide. During that week, the children had gone back to being with their mother and again appeared to distance themselves from him. It appeared as if the positive experience of that precious holiday week of being together had never happened.

One cannot know if at this point his mind was firmly made up to proceed with the act, but I do know that on the Wednesday before that fateful Saturday, he obtained potassium chloride from the pharmacy in his hospital, presumably for a patient.

On the Friday, a day before his suicide, Jonathan had dinner at our place. As mentioned, he was rather weary and not his usual courteous self when talking to his colleagues at the hospital, who were paging him as he was on call. But something strange happened. We had arranged for him to pick me up at

5 pm the following day to take me to the Selected Children's Award presentation evening, organised by the school, to see his ten-year-old child receive an award.

On his way out, Jonathan took out two tickets for the evening and put them on the sideboard. I was puzzled. "Why are you giving them to me? Aren't you picking me up?" I asked. He mumbled something about having received too many tickets. It didn't make much sense to me at the time. But who is a mere mother to question her authoritative son?

There was further evidence of his planning and preparation. A couple of weeks after my son's suicide, I met his secretary, as I wanted to hear from her any detail that would help me understand. She told me about her knowledge that the seeds of suicide are usually sown some time before the act. Once they are sown, very little can be done to prevent it happening, since the potential suicide cleverly disguises his intention. She repeated what she had written in the statement to police, that Jonathan had made sure before his holiday, and afterwards, that his in-tray was cleared. On the morning of the Friday before his death, he had been exceedingly cheerful and talked with her about making a date to celebrate their ten years of working together. Such cheerfulness, I learned, is characteristic of suicides who, having made their decision, experience a sense of relief and even exhilaration. For some, in fact, the decision has a calming effect. They have found a solution to how to escape their pain.

Jonathan had a logical mind, so part of the planning would have entailed selecting the place and means for the lethal act. The choice of his rooms at the hospital where he was a senior physician, his home away from home, made sense and is characteristic of doctors who suicide in familiar surroundings. The means, injection with potassium chloride, again was something he well understood as a cardiologist. As he did not work at this venue on weekends, he would have been confident there would not have been anyone there on a Saturday. He could carry out his plan without a risk of anybody interfering. And he did.

After writing about the relevance of planning to actual suicide behaviour, I came across another point of view. Kasia, now 56 years old, had been diagnosed as bipolar when she was in her thirties. She revealed how in a number of suicide attempts, she had made careful plans on what to do to escape her wretched feelings. The plans included jumping off a bridge and practising stepping over the rails; throwing herself under a train when it was rounding a curve; and swimming out to sea in the late evening. In each case, what stopped her from completing the act was the thought of how finding her body would affect her very young family members and her sick father. In these instances, she was able to think outside herself. But there were times when there was no plan. As she put it, she felt inhabited by the sickness; by a relentless sense of her brain eating itself, a sense that an outside force was controlling her and physically made her walk up to a steep lookout. Fortunately, while climbing towards the lookout she heard another voice telling her that she was a strong woman, that she was able to live, and that voice won. Kasia went on to live a most productive life from which many people have benefited.

So again, in unravelling the complex web of suicide, it is hard to make generalisations. One can only focus on how different threads of vulnerability interact in a particular person under specific circumstances.

18

What is it About Men?

The primary predictor of suicide is male gender. In Australia, the proportion of male suicides to women is 3:1. Similarly, the Samaritans Suicide Statistics Report shows that men in the United Kingdom are three times more likely to take their lives than women. And those aged between 45 and 49 have the highest rate of all – nearly four times that of women of the same age (Rudd, p.11).

In the United States, white males have a suicide rate much higher than those for any other gender or ethnic group, and it has been rising dramatically over the last few decades.

Zimmerman (Quadrant Online, 2020) cited a study by Princeton academics which found that the suicide rate for middle-aged white men jumped by 40 per cent in recent times as compared with decline in death rate for blacks and Hispanics. The reasons for the rise were thought to include the unfair legal treatment perceived by white males to be due to a jaundiced judicial system, in particular family courts, as well as different cultural expectations.

Another report cited by Zimmerman shows that in the United Kingdom, in the period 1981–2020, the rate of female suicide fell dramatically – by 50 per cent – while white male suicide rose dramatically. White men now account for 77 per cent of all suicides in the country. From the report it appears that white men are less likely to receive the protection of the law and are much less socially successful than almost every other ethnic-social group.

In this chapter I explore what it is about men that explains these statistics. And by chance I came across Matt Rudd's book, Man Down: Why Men Are Unhappy and What We Can Do About It (2020). Its recent publication could not have come at better time. His observations give a clear illustration of what research has shown about the experience of being a man in Western society.

Numerous studies in the Western world on socialisation of boys and girls indicate some fundamental differences between them. If one walks onto any school playground, one notices that boys tend to mix in more extended groups, mainly around sport activities, and girls sit or play in small more intimate groups, with chatting to each other the primary activity. Of course there are boys who are not included in the sport activity and girls who are excluded from the girls' small circle, and they suffer from the exclusion.

Traditionally, boys have been expected to grow into adults

who will go out into the world and do something, achieve something, so they can become the providers, the breadwinners. In other words, men need to construct their male identity. In modern times there is the equivalent expectation for women to achieve and become self-supporting. Entry of women into the workforce and increasingly, participation at the highest levels, has become the norm, which I applaud. However, any woman has the choice to decide her identity on the basis that she is biologically equipped to bear children. She can rely on her gender as a basis for her identity. There have been changes in societal expectation of men and women, with some men taking the role of child-rearing while women are the primary breadwinners, but they have not borne the children.

Both genders have new freedoms to not follow their prescribed gender roles but, as Rudd points out, all those newly found freedoms come with rules and conditions. The ritualised process of becoming a man is confined within a narrow set of parameters.

Since the beginning of Homo sapiens, men have taken the role of hunters and nomads, the ones who set up agricultural settlements, who built cities, who built the pyramids, while women did the domestic duties of keeping home, preparing food, and most importantly, raising children. Their job was not less significant but different. Men needed to be physically and emotionally strong, to be combative to carry out their role. I am describing patriarchal society. In modern times, when jobs in a whole variety of enterprise no longer need physical strength and gender is irrelevant, both our society and its structures are moving away from the patriarchal model.

The deeply embedded traditional expectation that man need to be stoic, strong, rational and unemotional is expressed in Rudyard Kipling's 'If':

"If you can keep your head when all about you
Are losing theirs ...
If you can make one heap of all your winnings,
And risk it all one turn of pitch-and-toss,
And lose, and start again at your beginnings ...
If you can meet with Triumph and Disaster.
And treat those two impostors just the same ...
You'll be a Man, my son!"

This type of man did not show his feelings, at least not verbally. Sharing how you felt, especially negative emotions, such as fear and distress and above all despair, was and unfortunately still is not what men do. It was not masculine behaviour.

Are the differences between men and women due to heredity or genetic factors? The one stable statistical difference between the genders evident from babyhood is aggression, associated with testosterone, the male hormone. It needs to be noted that statistical differences compare the middle 50 per cent on the normal curve of each group. At each end of the spectrum, 25 per cent of men would be very high or low in aggression and the same would apply to women. So, there are men low on aggression in their genetic make-up that runs counter to the norm of the combative man, but are still measured and, more importantly, measure themselves against the stereotype.

Does the shift from the patriarchal model, very recent in terms of human history, show in our deepest set expectations and attitudes towards males in our more gender equal society?

Rudd, in talking to men of his age – in their forties – noted the number who should be asking for help and sharing their feelings but choose to hide in a bath or block out their emotion (p.60). Displaying your feelings is still thought by many men as a weakness – not male. In fact, Rudd admits that in spite of his research and writing, he found himself saying to his son: 'Boys don't cry'.

I was astounded when talking to a friend who had been unhappy in his marriage for a number of years. All his friends were acutely aware of his situation and felt for him. He has an open, extravert personality, most sociable with many male friends, whom he meets regularly. So, when I asked him if he had talked about his feelings to his close friends, it was a surprise to hear him say quite forcefully: 'Oh, no. This was my private business!' Another friend, of similar stable background and disposition, also replied to the question whether he would talk to friends if he were in extreme distress with: 'Oh no, I like to solve my own problems.' This is exactly what Jonathan said to his brother when the latter offered: 'Talk to me, let me help you.' He did solve his problem his way, but what a tragic solution with devastating consequences.

This attitude of self-reliance reflects the notion that men are brought up to be independent. This expectation has high costs. Harvard Professor Carol Gilligan, whose lectures I attended, proposed an accurate picture of how a major relationship breakdown affects men. A man appears to stand strong and independent in his world but, in fact, at his base, there is a complex web of relationships, of interconnections, that support him. He may or may not be aware of what it is that holds him up, but when that network is torn apart, he collapses.

In contrast, in similar circumstances of unhappiness, relationship breakdown with its heavy financial and emotional costs, I, and quite a number of close female friends, confided in each other openly and frequently. For us, sharing is natural behaviour. What were friends for, after all? Again, in generalising one needs to keep in mind the women who are at the other end of the spectrum and value their privacy above all.

Men continue to show a reluctance to display emotion. In their eyes, it is a sign of weakness. Stoicism is still an indicator of masculinity. Their privacy, a critical factor in completed suicide, as discussed in Chapter 12, continues to operate. A father wrote that his surviving son, who is still very upset after his brother's suicide, lets the family see his distress only very rarely. He agonised: "Why are we (men) supposed to be so macho about these things?" (Woolley, p.41)

In a panel discussion on ABC Life Matters on 15 June 2021, during Men's Health Week, the question whether vulnerability and masculinity can co-exist was raised. Men, like all human beings, are vulnerable in times of personal or professional crises, but in spite of the fact that social rules are changing, they continue to struggle with connecting to their emotions and expressing them. Yet, the two experts on the panel emphasised that social connections can have a positive impact on men's health.

I understand also that men may often operate in competitive and combative work and social environments, where display of emotions would disadvantage them. That is certainly so in the medical profession.

It is likely that when we lived in smaller communities surrounded by extended families, there would be more opportunity to share your feelings with a grandparent, an aunt, a cousin – someone outside your nuclear family in which you have been socialised.

Author Robert Dessaix noted in his book The Time of Our Lives (2020), that marriage sometimes increases a man's or woman's isolation in our individualistic society, whereas in places like Java, life is unthinkable without a partner embedded with you in an endless network of family relationships. In fact, there is a suggestion in research that today a man in distress is more likely to talk to a close friend, male or female, rather than to the closed circle of his family. Journalist Amos Aikman reported the insight of a woman involved in the Darwin Youth Suicide Prevention Network, a community-based initiative. She herself had lost a very close friend to suicide. She stated: "I know as a mum … that my kids are going to talk to each other, to their cousins or other relatives, before they come and talk to me" (The Australian, 12 October 2020). The initiative aims to equip young people to support each other and contact appropriate services.

In an encouraging development, men are fighting back against the traditional view that showing emotion is a weakness. The most optimistic development in recent decades has been the growth of men's group movements. The men's groups create networks where the members are trained to share emotions. On the Life Matters program, a member of Beyond Blue, an organisation that provides a free online and telephone helpline for people with mental health issues, said that grassroots mental health groups have a lot to offer men.

I decided to investigate some men's groups with the thought that if only my son and the other young people I came across had been part of such a group, they may have been swayed from their act. They may have been exposed to other ideas of how to go on living with their pain, other ideas on how to react.

The first man I talked to was Bill. He is a 54-year-old, happily married man with young children, who has been the leader of a man's group from his late twenties, well before marriage. He explained that many Australian schoolboys connect through sport – a framework for camaraderie, sharing joint interest that often continues into early and even late adulthood. He was not sporty, did not belong and on the whole preferred the company of girls.

His search for what it meant to be a man made him aware that men were expected to be goal-oriented, rational, grounded and with clarity of purpose. He did not identify with this prescribed notion of masculinity. He did not fit the picture of the alpha male.

His search led him to the formation of a small group of men who would connect with each other in an open, non-judgemental way. Bill's group, with an age range of 18 to 65, meets for two hours every two weeks. The meeting starts with each man checking in for about seven to ten minutes, expressing whatever is on their mind, followed by reflection by the other members of the group, which often provides other perspectives. The essence of the group is trust – a basis for intimacy. For me, the key point is that the structure of men's groups does not allow for unhappiness to remain hidden. What a way out of the tunnel of the thinking of the would-be-suicide!

Sanjeev's story of how he came to be a member of a men's group is quite different. Sanjeev is 52 years old, married with children. He suffered from sex addiction and, as he said, he was full of anger arising from his relationship with his father. His psychologist suggested that he join a men's group. His first experience was at a three-day retreat, which takes place once a year. The main purpose of the retreat was to firstly support each man without judgement and secondly, to caringly confirm them if they were not true to themselves. Encouraged, Sanjeev joined a group of eight men who have been meeting for twelve years. The structure is similar to Bill's group. The fundamental basis of the group is trust. At the check-in, members respond to the questions: 'What is happening? What are your feelings? How are you coping?' The aim is to allow men to open up and show their vulnerability. Again, a powerful statement that is so counter to what our society has traditionally ascribed to being a man. Their answer to the question, 'Can vulnerability and masculinity co-exist?' is a definite yes.

My conversation with Lance, aged 60, added another perspective on men's groups. He explained that men's groups developed out of active face-to-face therapeutic groups that grew and proliferated in the 1970s, though some had much older origins, such as Alcoholics Anonymous. These groups included narcotics addiction, sex addiction and various personal growth therapies. The transition of mixed gender groups to men only was partly a backlash from feminism but above all, it fulfilled a need by men to be in a safe, non-judgemental place among other men, where issues of relationships and where despair, anger and lots of angst could be safely expressed.

The mental health service Are You Bogged, Mate? targets men in rural and remote communities across Australia. Mary O'Brien said she started the organisation by accident after she wrote an article following two suicides in her local area. "The opinion piece went viral and then people started to ask me to come and talk at events," she said. When she started doing research, she didn't like what she found. Now Ms O'Brien travels to rural and remote Australia talking to men and women. Her aim is to break down the stigma while normalising that everybody goes through patches and that everybody gets bogged.

The benefits of men's groups for would-be-suicides are obvious. At the time of writing this book, however, a men's movement is as yet not part of mainstream culture. It is still an unlikely option for many men who find themselves in a state of utter unhappiness and despair, who do not choose to turn to a professional therapist, who are locked in a Sealed Box.

Providing spaces and places for men to share their emotions needs to become a national objective. It needs to be promoted as a totally acceptable activity.

19

A Historical Perspective

Suicide, like all human behaviour, takes places in a particular social, cultural and religious context and in a specific historical period. Although at first I did not consider looking at the broader context of suicide, once I started reading in the area, its relevance became obvious. I have also come to appreciate the ongoing influence of older beliefs on how we – and that includes the young people who take their lives – view the act.

The word suicide did not appear in Samuel Johnson's dictionary of 1755. Prior to its use, the act was termed as self-murder, self-destruction, self-killing, and self-homicide. The word suicide, the deliberate killing of oneself, is probably an English coinage from 1728. It originated in 1650s, from Latin suicidium, suicide, from Latin sui, of oneself and cidium, a killing.

Tatz & Tatz have written on how suicide has gone through any number of phases, treatments, punishments, legal controls, philosophic permutations, moral judgements, religious reforms and geographical shifts. Whatever the circumstances, however, when an individual has the strength to go against the inherent all-powerful instinct to cling to life, they do so for their own reasons.

In some warrior societies where the ideal is bravery, suicide is looked upon as an act of honour. For example, suttee was a largely historical practice found chiefly among Hindus in the northern and pre-modern regions of South Asia, in which a widow sacrificed herself by sitting on top of her deceased husband's funeral pyre.

Suttee was the ideal of womanly devotion held by certain Brahman and royal castes. Women sometimes suffered immolation before their husbands' expected death in battle. Rajputs also practised jauhar, which was suicide to save women from rape at the hands of conquering enemies, which they considered worse than death.

In a number of ancient cultures, such as Egypt, it was the custom for the slaves and soldiers of a departed king to kill themselves in order to accompany their dead king to an afterlife, but I doubt they had a choice.

In Ancient Greece, Homer recorded self-killing as something natural and usually heroic. Enumerating a number of specific cases, Alvarez concluded that the Ancient Greeks took their own lives solely for understandable – by contemporary standards – reasons, such as grief, patriotic principle or to avoid dishonour. The keys were moderation and high principle.

This attitude is still evident today, as one hears of company leaders and politicians in both Western and Asian countries who resign and then kill themselves in the face of loss of honour or loss of reputation. They do not want to live shamed and as outcasts in their world. In the fifth century BC, the Greek philosopher Plato thought that suicide was justified and rational if life became intolerable, such as suffering a painful disease or other constraints. And, of course, the notion of intolerable is subjective. What may be tolerable to one is intolerable to others. I suspect tolerance depends on how thick- or thin-skinned one is. Sensitive people are, by definition, more vulnerable. This view certainly has echoes in contemporary culture. For the Greeks, all that was required was to plead their reason before the senate and obtain official permission. 'If your existence is hateful to you, die; if you are bowed with grief, abandon life.' (Alvarez, p.53)

I have referred to the Roman view, as put by Cicero, that suicide delivered an acceptable end to pain and dotage, an end without stigma or shame. Romans saw suicide as a carefully considered action that validated the way they had lived their lives. At a time when euthanasia is being increasingly accepted as a humane action, when most of us have come to accept that we are free to choose to have an abortion as our bodies belong to us, the Roman approach appears acceptable. But then I have come to realise that in Ancient Rome, death was casual and public, and large audiences cheered the spectacle of gladiators butchering each other. In that period it appeared that suicide was a noble act when performed by the upper classes, but the enslaved were not granted the privilege of choice.

What we still think of as honourable suicide includes situations when a whole group chooses death to stay true to a moral principle, such as the hundreds of Jews who put themselves to death in the fortress of Masada, rather than submit to the invading Roman legions who would have forced them to give up their religion. The Judaeo-Christian belief that banned suicide, a view held by the early Christians, became perverted during the late Roman and early Middle Ages.

I found Alvarez's discussion of the not only approved but venerated suicide in the name of martyrdom interesting. It appears that the would-be-martyrs sought to die and often provoked death in order to achieve martyrdom, accompanied on their way by admiring crowds. Martyrdom was a Christian creation as much as a Roman persecution of early Christians (p.580). The early Christian fathers offered posthumous glory; the martyrs were celebrated in the Church calendar; their death officially recorded; their relics worshipped. Suicide, thinly disguised as martyrdom in the name of God, offered certain redemption. I suspect, however, that this type of lethal self-injury, where one expects to move to a heavenly realm and be rewarded for this so-called self-sacrificial action, is vastly different for those who see death as a terminal end. It would appear that the latter requires much more courage, though one cannot know whether parting from this earthly life was not equally daunting for the martyrs.

This phase came to an end when it got out of hand, with too many young people choosing martyrdom as an attractive option to earthly life. In the thirteenth century, St Thomas Aquinas in his Summa Theologica declared that suicide is a mortal sin against God. He saw it as a sin against justice – the individual's responsibilities to his community – and a sin against charity – the instinctive charity each person bears towards themselves. But, perversely, the Christian ban on suicide founded on respect for life and concern for the suicide's soul, finished off as the legislated sanction for atrocities by which the body of the suicide was degraded – they would be deprived of a religious burial, their goods forfeited and their memory defamed. I read about this horrific barbarity towards the suicide with great distress.

The Judaeo-Christian tradition views each human body as the vehicle for an immortal soul, which will be judged not in this world but the next. Since life is the gift of God, to reject it is to reject Him, his will. In pre-modern times, a Jewish suicide was buried in unconsecrated ground and no prayers, tributes or eulogies were offered on their behalf. Modern Jewish and Christian practice allow a suicide a regular burial, taking a softer approach if there are indications of mental illness, which in today's medical paradigm, they are always deemed to have. By the nineteenth century, following the Enlightenment and scientific revolution, suicide became less of a moral and religious question and more of a social and medical matter. The label of insanity became preferable to the disgrace attaching to someone who wittingly ended their life. The abolition of the legal penalties happened over time. In England, the laws concerning the confiscation of property were not changed until 1870, and an unsuccessful suicide could still go to prison until 1960 (Alvarez, p.43). The phrase *suicide while the balance of his mind was disturbed* was developed by lawyers as a protection against these laws. I wonder if the current reliance on mental health professionals to deal with the complex phenomenon of suicide derives from this early association between suicide and lunacy. When I told a friend, married to a psychiatrist, of Jonathan's taking his life, her immediate response, knowing nothing about the circumstances was: 'Oh, he must have had a psychotic moment'. Another example of the legacy of this period is the phrase 'committed suicide'. Committed, as in committed a crime or committed treason? People die of many causes, but we don't think they committed death. In the case of self-death, the term used is commit. Why? They cease to live, just like every other young or old person, be it in car accidents or disease or other misadventure, like we all do at some stage of our lives. It appears that suicide still carries the stigma attached to it from earlier times.

20

Contemporary Cultural Context

Modern suicide has been removed from the vulnerable, volatile world of human beings and hidden away in the isolation wards of science (Alvarez, p.61).

Suffering is an integral part of the human condition. People in all ages and cultures have had to live through poverty, starvation, cataclysmic events of destruction by other humans and nature, and personal tragedies. In the last and current century, they have had to suffer through the terrors of trench warfare of World War I, the Depression, the atrocities of World War II, and now are living with and dying from COVID-19 in the pandemic.

According to Victor Frankl, suffering is an ineradicable part of life … without suffering and death, human life cannot be complete. In Buddhism the first of their Four Noble Truths is that life is about suffering, pain and misery. People over ages have suffered and endured. Existential distress is just that. It is often terrible and terrifying – and normal.

The contemporary notion that life is about happiness has its roots in the American culture. The American Declaration of Independence of 1776 laid down the unalienable right to life, liberty and the pursuit of happiness. However, as a wise American psychologist explained to me, it has been misinterpreted as a right to happiness rather than the pursuit of. In their chapter 'The Aspirin Age', Tatz & Tatz developed the theme of how in the interwar years Americans – and the rest of the world – lived through a time of a lot of misery, unemployment, poverty, extreme ideologies such as the Ku Klux Klan and anti-Semitism.

Following this period, the shortage of happiness came to be diagnosed as a sign of unwellness that needed to be cured by drugs such as Aspirin and, in Australia, a Bex and a good lie down, or by mental health practitioners. The fact that existential distress and pain are part of human life, more acute for some than others and more evident at certain periods of one's life, was no longer accepted. Distress was no longer something one had to bear. One needed to be positive and optimistic, a belief that has led to the development of Positive Psychology. One no longer faced problems but rather challenges, which presumably could be solved with the right tools. While I can appreciate the merits of seeing the glass half full rather than half empty at all times, it does not fit the reality of many people's real life situations.

I came across an example of the American emphasis on the positive on a visit to the Norman Rockwell Museum in the United States a couple of years ago. Norman Perceval Rockwell was a twentieth-century American author, painter and illustrator, whose work is loved by Americans for its reflection of American culture. However, it was not a reflection of the reality of that culture but its idealised version. His paintings appeared on the cover of the Saturday Evening Post, where he worked continuously for 47 years. This period covered both world wars and the Great Depression, yet the images were consistently about the positives of everyday American lives, so different from their European counterparts. During the period of American involvement in World War II, Rockwell created a series of covers featuring the recruit Willie Gillis, a fictional character, which describe the life of the typical American boy from the first day in uniform to his happy return home from the war. Rockwell chose not to paint combat images, focusing more on the soldier's ideal than on the harshness of war.

Within this context of positive thoughts, of optimistic images, there is no place for the hurt, anguish, soreness, psychological pain or using Shneidman's (1995) term, psychache of the would-be-suicide or a deeply unhappy person. Tatz & Tatz quoted American sociologist Allan Horwitz and social work specialist Jerome Wakefield, who lamented the loss of sadness and deplored the way in which psychiatry has turned normal sorrow into a depressive disorder. Suicide was deemed to be a consequence of a disturbed mind and thus became the domain of the medical profession. The Holy Grail remains biological intervention, the magic pill, the antidepressant that dulls suicidal thoughts, behaviours and actions.

But the prevailing view of medication as a frontline treatment is now being questioned. When looked at from a historical perspective, though there have been indescribable changes in the way society functions, in scientific and technological knowledge, in our values, it is clear that suicide is a human act by an individual for which, in the most part, there is a reason.

When it occurs, its reality is introspectively undeniable. Suicide occurs when the psychache is deemed by that person to be unbearable. This means that suicide also has to do with different individual thresholds for enduring psychological pain.

I now wonder to what extent my son and the other young ones who took their precious lives were influenced by the expectation that life is about being happy, that psychache is not part of the normal human condition; not truly understanding, not accepting the notion that existential distress and pain are part of human life. They are something that one has to bear, with the support of family, friends and community.

The above discussion has taken a psychological perspective. The philosophical perspective offers another view of the contemporary human condition. Jonathan Sacks, in his book Morality (2020), highlights a survey of how Americans find meaning in life, published by the Pew Research Center in 2018. Respondents indicated that the most important source of meaning in their life was family. Other sources included career, money, friends, hobbies, activities and religious faith. Another survey of college students found that whereas in the 1960s their top priority was developing a meaningful life, in the 2000s it was being very well off financially. There were a number of responses that told of lives of despair. Most of the responses focused on what made people feel good about themselves, what gave satisfaction to the self.

In a chapter on 'Meaning,' Sacks recounts the reaction by

two distinguished American philosophers, Dreyfus and Kelly, to the suicide at the age of 46, of David Foster Wallace, one of the finest American writers of his generation. For Wallace mere existence in the contemporary world was unbearably empty. Dreyfus and Kelly saw the way he spoke about his life and his lethal self-injury as something of wider significance about the cultural discontent of contemporary culture. Wallace's view spoke directly to how difficult it is to find meaning in a life without a dimension of the sacred or, as others have put it, of living without a god.

David Brooks described the distracted frame of mind that occurs when you have too many open options: when everything is available, every lifestyle on offer, when all you have freedom, but nothing to guide you in that freedom (Sacks, p.243).

As an older, wise friend who had a faith said: 'We are too little to fill our lives.' We need commitment to something beyond our selves to give us a sense that our life has meaning. It requires reaching out beyond one's self, be it toward a meaning to fulfil, or toward another human being lovingly to encounter (Frankl, p.90).

With a decline in religion and a decline in faith generally, it is harder to find that something in the contemporary secular, materialistic culture. I can well understand why young people so passionately embrace climate change and threats to the ecology of our earth as causes beyond their selves.

It is hard to suffer when that suffering has no meaning. Yet meaning can be found, as Einstein expressed it so well:

Strange is our situation here on earth. Each of us comes for a short visit, not knowing why, yet sometimes seeming to divine purpose. From the standpoint of daily life, however, there is one thing we do know: that man is here for the sake of other men – above all for those upon whose smiles and well-being our own happiness depends (Sacks, p.251).

Applying the discussion of our contemporary cultural context to the young people who killed themselves, it is difficult to attribute their decision directly to the times they lived in. But it is likely that the notion that unhappiness is not a normal part of life, did contribute to their decision. Moreover, growing up in self-centred times, without any given causes or commitments that would have made them feel that their lives were worthy, these young people did not have the extra buffer to resist the urge to die.

I do not know of the background of the sons and daughters of my respondents, but thinking of Jonathan, he did have a deep commitment to medicine, and devoted years of studying, researching and long hours of work to healing his fellow human beings. Yet this was not enough.

21

What We Can do to
Save Young Lives

In my attempt to understand the different aspects of suicide by exploring relevant research, philosophy, literature, reading first-hand accounts by bereaved parents and in-depth interviews of some of them, I have learned one thing – suicide is not unthinkable.

I did not know that suicide or lethal self-injury is the biggest single leading cause of death in Australians aged 15 to 44. I did not know that men are three times as likely to complete the act of suicide. Each year, approximately 3000 Australians take their own life and 65,000 attempt suicide.

Suicide is a response to intense psychache – hurt, anguish and psychological pain, in the mind of an individual. Suicide has a purpose: it is intentional death. The person deciding to take their life makes a conscious choice of the best possible practical solution to a problem, crisis or desperation that is perceived as intolerable. Their despair is intolerable because they experience some intensely felt psychological needs which are not being met.

Desire to liberate oneself from pain appears to be the immediate reason. Individuals planning suicide as an escape from life find themselves in what Tatz & Tatz have called a sealed box. They do not see, nor do they seem to want to hear, of other perspectives, of other options. That is why prevention of suicide is such a challenge.

Research has identified two basic human needs which, when not met, contribute to the desire for death or rather, the wish to stop living. One is a thwarted sense of belongingness. No matter how loved, when an individual perceives they have lost connection to those who are central in their lives, they experience a sense of social isolation – which is unbearable for most of us.

Perceived burdensomeness is the other basic threat, which when identified puts one at risk. It appears that at the heart of suicide is the belief that one's life has no value, that one is worthless. Thinking of one's self as ineffective is associated with thinking that one is a burden to one's loved ones and that, in fact, taking one's life would relief them of the burden. From the perspective of the would-be suicide, it is an act of altruism.

There is no single cause of suicide. In the background of the young people who take their lives is a complex web of interactions between unmet psychological needs within an individual, their personal characteristics, specific circumstances, the interactions embedded within a wider cultural and social context.

Though we are paying much more attention and providing funding for the prevention of suicide, our knowledge of completed acts of lethal self-injury and what to do to reduce their occurrence is inadequate. The type of commitment that our society at all levels and across the board institutions, including the media, have made in areas such as the anti-smoking campaign, stopping the evils of child abuse and domestic violence needs to be also directed at prevention of suicide of our young.

We require much more focused and fine-grained studies, modelled on that by the Australia's National Research Organisation for Women's Safety on the killing of a woman by her intimate ex- or current partner. Such research which would identify a common sequence of events, interactions and relationship dynamics in the weeks, days and moments leading up to lethal self-injury, would yield some useful information. It would indicate that we, as a society, are committed to the prevention of all those lives unlived in deed and not just in words.

Personality is a key factor in the decision to complete suicide. Developing a profile of the type of personality and temperamental variables that make one more vulnerable would be a significant step in identifying potential suicides.

Moreover, the information we do have needs to be part of our common knowledge. For example, the devastating impact of a person's suicide not only on their children, parents, siblings but also the wider community, needs to be part of our public conversation. One needs to understand that ripples of the event, which still has a stigma attached to it, extend across generations. Just perhaps, if this effect was well known, the young people planning to lethally self-injure may hesitate to complete the act.

Above all, we as a community need to take on board the

fact that suicide is largely a man's issue. Although the statistics are published and known, the question of why this is so is rarely addressed. The fact that men die by suicide three times as much as women requires much more community attention and research. Indeed, there seems to be reluctance in the public domain to even acknowledge this gender imbalance.

Community awareness of the fact that male gender is the biggest predictor of suicide could be raised by media; incorporated in the shows we watch, in community platforms; in discussions such as presentations of New Ideas, just the way there has been a considerable increase in community exposure to and awareness of transgender, LGBTQIA and Indigenous perspectives.

We are living at a time where women's voices seem to get a ready hearing. As a feminist myself, I understand and support this after centuries of dominant male voices within patriarchal societies. But I am also a mother and grandmother of sons and grandsons, and I want to hear their voices too. The voices of the successful, macho men in business and government and politics still dominate society, and domestic physical violence by men still damages the lives of women and children. But what about the voices of the more gentle men, the men who care passionately about their families and their children, who contribute to their communities in so many ways, but who do not shout their concerns?

Our society has made fighting against the prevalence of domestic violence a priority, though it still is an uphill battle. The definition of domestic violence means that in a relationship or marriage, one or both of the partners use physical, sexual, emotional or psychological abuse and violence, which affect both women and men. This includes belittling one's partner, making them feel worthless, often in front of the children, to the children's detriment. The old term was subjecting someone to mental cruelty. And cruelty it is. As noted, a sense of one's worthlessness is a significant contributor to suicidal ideation. The fact that according to the ABS Personal Safety Survey data (2016) close to half the victims of emotional abuse were men, is rarely addressed in the public domain. Their voices need to be heard.

Britain-based Matt Rudd, in Man Down, dealt with some of the challenges men in contemporary Western society are confronting. He pointed out that on the surface, men today don't have much to complain about. Yet beneath the surface, it's a different story. An alarming number of men end up feeling anxious, depressed and exhausted, yet reluctant to admit they are.

As noted, men who find themselves overwhelmed by psychological pain, who are in anguish, are unlikely to share their feelings with their family and friends. It is just not what men do. Their despair is hidden. One of the promising developments in recent decades is the formation of men's groups. In these groups men learn to trust their fellow members and feel safe to talk about their psychological pain and get feedback on ways to help them live.

Men's groups are still considered a fringe movement and not quite what a seemingly successful man in a high status profession such as medicine, the judiciary or government would be likely to attend. A public campaign that aims at making belonging and participating in a men's group mainstream, as acceptable as going out for a game of golf or to watch football, would be a valuable initiative.

Breakdown of a major relationship emerges as a significant immediate context in lethal self-injury. This one factor is in the background of most of the reports of my respondents. It increases one's vulnerability to succumbing to psychological pain.

Recognition by society that men are particularly vulnerable and at risk during the period of separation and divorce is imperative. The painful and often prolonged process of separation and divorce, involving family court proceedings, separation from home and the threatened loss of connection with one's children are major factors in thwarting one's deep need of belongingness.

As I cited in Chapter 8, Dr David Curl wrote how during separation and divorce, apart from experiencing grief, anger or confusion, the most important things in a parent's life are at risk: their home, financial security and relationship with their children. This applies particularly to dads, who are usually expected to move out of the family home and therefore lose the day-to-day contact with their kids. These losses explain why men are particularly vulnerable at this time.

Curl makes the point that in this period, all participants need support services. The focus should be on the children's needs, which must be paramount, but the vulnerabilities of their fathers and mothers also require attention. This is a red flag period for suicide attempts and successful suicides, yet there are no targeted support services available for the parents.

My exploration of factors related to the devastating phenomenon of young people fatally injuring themselves supports Curl's passionate plea for society to recognise that divorce and separation are not only a legal but also mental health and social issues. There is a parallel in other moments of vulnerability in human life, such as guidance for gamblers, alcoholics and drug addicts, which are recognised as health as well as legal issues.

I understand that the intersection of legal and mental health issues poses a challenge for Family Court judges. While trained in the legal and procedural issues involved, do the judges understand the mental health impact of their orders and the way they are interpreted in real life, on the participants? The adverse impact on the mental health of the separating partners would apply particularly in cases of high-level dispute and emotion, which by their very nature signify a red flag. Judges and all parties involved, including divorce lawyers, must be trained in this area, which requires more hard data. The Family Court needs to take this into account and address the issue directly.

Educational campaigns to raise awareness of other social contexts that contribute to individuals' vulnerability to suicide are loss of job, living in rural or remote communities and challenges of being part of specific professions such as medicine. Raised awareness would lead to further action to determine specific risk factors and required action.

At this stage, research has identified some personality characteristics associated with completed suicide. They include difficulty in expressing and communicating negative emotions; a high threshold of privacy; and physical courage – each of the characteristics found more in men than women, be it for cultural or genetic reasons. The evidence suggests that would-be-suicides, once they have decided and planned their action, do not want to be stopped in their exit option. Those with high privacy threshold as part of their personality certainly are even more unlikely to disclose their suicidal ideation and plans. This is one major reason why their families, those closest to them agonise: We did not see it coming.

What can families do? Those close to a loved one who has taken their life admit that in hindsight, they had noticed changes in behaviour in the preceding period, such as with-drawal, weight loss, no longer being excited by things that pre-viously made them feel enthusiastic – behaviours that can be explained as fatigue or just feeling down. No matter how obser-vant the parent may be, any probing by them is usually firmly rejected, as my son's 'Come off it, Mum', indicated. However, not interfering is not what we necessarily need to do.

I quote the wise words of my respondent Nora: "Not to say 'I can't do it for you, it has to be you' to my son who was self-medicating with alcohol on top of his official medications." The troubled person already knows this all too well, and needs to hear something like: I know you don't feel strong enough to do this on your own, but hang on to me and we'll do it together.

In my interview with Kasia, who had described to me her suicide attempts, she admitted that she was actively pushing her family away. She now had the insight and advice to parents and close family members: 'Do not allow yourself to be pushed away'. We have no proof that this would have any preventative effect, but it is thought provoking and requires further exploration.

In fact, there is a suggestion in research that a man in dis-tress is more likely to disclose his pain to a close friend, male or female, a cousin, or workmate or acquaintance than to the close circle of his family. The initiative of the Darwin Youth Suicide Prevention Network aims to equip young people to support each other and contact appropriate services.

An impressive initiative in developing a suicide preven-tion strategy at work was reported by Ewin Hannan. Since people spend so much of their time at work, Suicide Prevention Australia, in conjunction with organisations such a Lifeline and Beyond Blue, have launched a national framework for suicide prevention in the workplace. It aims to equip managers with the skills to recognise when colleagues are in distress, while building the confidence of organisations to have conversations at work about suicide (The Australian, 22 June 2021). So, for example, when frontline managers identify signs in an employee such as behaviour changes, they can guide the worker to the appropriate support.

The biggest challenge for us as a society is to remove the stigma associated with suicide. Citing the Chief Executive of Suicide Prevention Australia: we seem to have got more confident speaking about issues to do with mental health, but suicide prevention still has a particular stigma, a particular fear associated with it (Hannan).

On a positive note, attitudes can change when a society makes a commitment to do so. Good examples of a concerted and successful societal change are our easy acceptance in recent times of homosexuality, transgender and same-sex marriage. This was achieved by harnessing all available attitude-changing resources at national and local level, such as printed and online media, movies, streaming services, and prominent people being outspoken about the relevant issues.

Suicide is a societal issue. Society must address it. I hope that the issues raised in this book will contribute to more comfortable conversations in the public domain on lethal self-injury by our young men and women, and ways to reduce its rate.

The journey in writing this book has been, at times, most painful, but it will have been a worthwhile one if it saves even one life.

Appendix

Responses to My Invitation to Share With Me

What I wish I had done. What can be done?

I would like to see a Mental Health class or Mental Health Curriculum in all high schools in Australia to let young people understand about mental health in the same way as physical health. Mental health is crucial in our daily survival to function normally and can include the foods that affect behaviour.

I tended to treat my son with respect as an adult. He was my last-born and I constantly resisted the temptation to still think of him as my baby. I was careful never to press too hard in a conversation even when I wanted more information and more clarity, so opportunities for him to share his despair with me fully never arose. This is probably the most troubling and disturbing question I am left with: in my efforts to give my youngest child space to go his own way, solve his own problems and forge his own path, did I make a terrible mistake?

Not to say 'I can't do it for you, it has to be you', to my son, who was self-medicating with alcohol on top of his official medications. I learned later from an experienced drug and alcohol counsellor never to say this. The troubled person already knows this all too well and needs to hear something like: 'I know you don't feel strong enough to do this on your own, but hang on to me and we'll do it together.' Of course, rationally and professionally, I know it is not that simple and that there were many factors involved. But as a mother, that is a conversation I would change.

If we can remove the stigma from suicide and mental health, people will feel much safer and will seek help. As a society we have to remove the taboos and educate ourselves so we can save our children.

Suicide is a public health issue, not a crime. Suicide is largely preventable and has an ethical dimension. Victims are driven by pain not choice. Stigmatising suicide with secrecy means that I cannot talk about these issues in a comfortable way to my family back home, for cultural and religious reasons.

I am very happy to assist you in your book and would not mind you using my name in it as a reference. I am all about raising awareness about mental health, and I do not hide away from it. In the last eight years as a mental health presenter, I have visited most schools in Sydney's south and spoken to thousands of students.

In regard to your request, for me there are certain things

I wish I had known. I would have wanted to know all about depression and mental health and the signs and symptoms, where to go for help. This information would have saved my son. He had all the markers for depression and in hindsight I can tick every single box on the symptoms checklist. But I knew nothing about it. I ran him around to various doctors and specialists and put him on all these different drug treatments for a physical illness. Not once did I stop and consider it may be a mental illness. I truly believe armed with that info and the proper tools in my mental health kit, I could have saved his life. In not having that knowledge I feel I failed my son, as I did not give him the help he really needed. And that guilt has caused my own mental health to suffer greatly.

Knowledge is a powerful thing. And using it correctly can change the course of things. I would wish all parents bereaved by suicide to have that knowledge. They may have no idea what caused their child to take his/her own life but with it they might be able to understand why. I know that this is very important to those left behind, answers! (Katrina Tsaftaropoulos)

For myself there are two things that stand out in answer to What I wish I had done. One is that I left organising a psychologist for Jonathan too late. I was going to tell him about it on the very evening of the day he took his life. I had suggested it on earlier occasions, only to be rebuffed. He did accept that it would be beneficial but was worried that visits to a psychologist may interfere with allotment of custody of his children by the Family Court, and also that it would have been unacceptable for his medical colleagues to know. It was only in that final week of his life that it occurred to me that if I paid for the visits, no one would know. I wish I had thought of this earlier.

The other thing is my response, or lack of it, to Jonathan's obvious loss of weight. Like the other mothers who have shared their regrets with me, I did talk to him about it. I was worried but did not press it when he brushed it – my 'nagging' – off with his customary gesture indicating 'You are pushing it, Mum'.

More specifically, I wish I had been alarmed by his off-the-scale score when I administered the Life Stress Inventory, which indicated that my son was at risk. If any of my clients had registered such a high score, I would have taken note and acted. But not on this occasion. Both of us laughed when I told him the score. Laughed? Did we, did I, think my son was invincible? That he had qualities that would allow him to overcome such immense pressures? I cannot understand.

I wish I'd had the knowledge to understand that my son was at risk. He was a gentle, non-combative man going through marriage breakdown and Family Court proceedings – a non-benign environment in which he did not function well. Access to and close relationship with his children, central to his life, were, in his mind, threatened. In addition there were professional concerns with the proposed changes in organisation of his hospital services, as well as financial pressures. He was naturally a very private person, who had difficulty expressing negative emotions. His profession of medicine did not allow for the display of anything but the at-all-times competent physician, the one who was in control, the one whose job it was to save others' lives, but not his own.

All the signs were there. I observed it all but did not understand.

The only explanation I have is my total ignorance of anything to do with suicide. There is now much more attention in the media and by governments addressing the scourge of young people taking their lives than there was at the time when my son lethally self-injured. But yet I am not sure ignorance is the only reason. It is more likely that suicide for me was unthinkable.

References

Aikman, Amos. Child Abuse, neglect to suicide risk factors. *The Australian*, 30 September 2020

Aikman, Amos. Knowing how to reach out when a troubled loved one needs your help. *The Australian*, 12 October 2020

Alvarez, Al. *The Savage God. A Study of Suicide.* Random House, 1972

Arndt, Bettina. *Men Too.* Wilson Publishing, 2018

Black, Dasia. *Letter from My Father.* Brandl & Schlesinger, 2012

Camus, Albert. *The Myth of Sisyphus.* London: Penguin Books, 2015

Curl, David. We can do without the combative family contests. *The Australian*, 2 January 2020

Curry, Andrew. Parents' emotional trauma may change their children's biology. Studies in mice show how. *Science*, 18 July 2019

Dessaix, Robert. *The Time of Our Lives.* Brio Books, 2020

Frankl, Viktor. *The Unheard Cry for Meaning.* New York: Washington Square Press, 1978

Golding, William. *Lord of the Flies.* Faber & Faber, 1954

Goldstein, Rebecca. *Betraying Spinoza. The Renegade Jew Who Gave Us Modernity* (Jewish Encounters Series). Schocken, 2006

Guttman, David. *Reclaimed Powers. Men and Women in Later Life.* Evanston, Illinois: Northwestern University Press, 1994

Hannan, Ewin. New suicide prevention strategy at work alerts managers to warning signs. *The Australian*, 22 June 2021

Hari, Johann. *Lost Connections: Uncovering the Causes of Depression and Unexpected Solutions*. London: Bloomsbury Circus, 2018

James, William. *The Principles of Psychology*. New York: Henry Holt & Company, 1890

Joiner, Thomas. *Why People Die by Suicide*. Harvard University Press, 2007

Kolves, Kairi; Milner, Allison; McKay, Kathy; Diego De Leo (Eds). *Suicide in Rural and Remote Areas of Australia*. Longueville Media, 2012

Linehan, Marsha. *Cognitive-behavioral Treatment of Borderline Personality Disorder*. New York: Guilford Press, 1993

McCormack, Anne. A perfect storm: towards reducing the risk of suicide in the medical profession. *Medical Journal of Australia*, 2018, p.209

Menninger, K.A. Purposive accidents as an expression of self-destructive tendencies. *International Journal of Psycho-Analysis*, 1936, 17, pp.6-16

O'Connor, Rory. *When it Is Darkest*. Penguin Books Australia, 2021

Pasternak, Boris. *An Essay in Autobiography*, trans. Manya Harari. London: Collins & Harrill Press, 1959, pp.91-93

Rudd, Matt. *Man Down: Why Men Are Unhappy and What We Can Do About It*. Little Brown, 2020

Sacks, Jonathan. *Morality*. New York: Basic Books, 2020

Shneidman, Edwin. *Suicide as psychache: A Clinical Approach to Self-Destructive Behavior*. Rowman & Littlefield, 1995

Suedfeld, Peter. Homo Invictus: The Indomitable Species. *Canadian Psychology/Psychologie Canadienne*, vol. 38, 3 August 1997, pp.164-73

Suedfeld, Peter. *Light from the Ashes*. University of Michigan Press, 2001

Tatz, Colin & Tatz, Simon. *The Sealed Box of Suicide. The Contexts of Self-Death*. Springer, 2019

Valent, Paul. *Heart of Violence: why people harm each other*. North Melbourne: Arden, 2020

Verghis, Sharon. Wounded Healers. *The Weekend Australian Magazine*, 5 May 2018

Woolley, Belinda (Ed). *If Only … personal stories of loss through suicide*. University of Western Australia Press, 2006

Yehuda, Rachel & Lehner, Amy. Intergenerational transmission of trauma effects: putative role of epigenetic mechanisms. *World Psychiatry,* vol. 17, 3 October 2018

Online references

ABS. National Survey of Mental Health and Wellbeing, 2007

ABS. Personal Safety, Australia. 2016

AIHW. Australia's Children. Web report, 3 April 2020

Carey, Tim & McPhee, Rob. It's despair, not depression that's responsible for Indigenous suicide. In the conversation.com, 14 December 2018

Costa, Dora, L, Yetter, Noelle & DeSomer, Heather. Intergenerational transmission of paternal trauma among US Civil War ex-POWs. PNAS October 30, 2018. 115 (44)11215-20

Harper, Hilary. What it means to be a man. ABC Radio National, *Life Matters*, 15 June 2021

Hinduja, D. & Patchin, J.W. Bullying, Cyberbullying and Suicide Statistics. Megan Meier. meganmeierfoundation, 2020

Yossi Levi-Belz et al. Mental Pain, Communication Difficulties, and Medically Serious Suicide Attempts: A Case-Control Study. *Archives of Suicide Research*, 18:1, 74-87, 2014. DOI: 10.1080/13811118.2013.809041

Levi Y, et al. Mental pain and its communication in medically serious suicide attempts: an 'impossible situation'. J Affect Disord 2008 Dec;111(2-3):244-50. DOI: 10.1016/j.jad.2008.02.022. Epub 2008 Apr 23

Miller, Jacob, N. & Black, Donald, W. Bipolar disorder and suicide: a Review – PubMed, 2020 Jan 18; 22 (2):6.doi: 10.1007/s11920-020-1130-0

National research organisations join forces to investigate patterns of intimate partner homicide and breaches of parenting orders. *The Australian,* 20 April 2020

SBS. Bullying's Deadly Toll. *The Feed.* 30 August 2016, 7.30 pm

Serani, Deborah. Bullycide. *Psychology Today*, June 2, 2018

Shneidman, E.S. & Farberow, N.L. The Los Angeles suicide prevention center: A demonstration of public health feasibilities. 1965 https://www.ncbi.nlm.nih.gov/pmc/articles/PMC1256136/pdf/amjphnation00153-0023.pdf

Zimmerman, Augusto. The unique discrimination white men face. *Quadrant Online*, 17 November 2020